# smart
## food

photography by Jean Cazals

quadrille

First published in 2004 by
**Quadrille Publishing Limited**
Alhambra House
27-31 Charing Cross Road
London WC2H OLS

Reprinted in 2005 (twice)
10 9 8 7 6 5 4 3

ISBN 1 84400 132 6

**Creative Director** Helen Lewis
**Editorial Director** Jane O'Shea
**Consultant Editor** Janet Illsley
**Photographic Direction** Vanessa Courtier
**Senior Designer** Jim Smith
**Editor** Jane Keskeys
**Production** Beverley Richardson

Printed in China

**Cookery notes**
All recipes serve 4 unless otherwise stated. All spoon measures are level
unless otherwise indicated. Follow either metric or imperial measures, not
a mixture of both as they are not necessarily interchangeable. Use fresh
herbs and freshly ground black pepper unless otherwise suggested.

# Contents

# smart
# starters

# Scallops with broad bean purée

12 large scallops, cleaned
3 tbsp extra virgin olive oil
salt and pepper
1 tbsp lemon juice
**For the broad bean purée**
100g/4oz broad beans
½ garlic clove, crushed

1 tbsp freshly grated Parmesan
  cheese
1 tbsp chopped fresh mint
2 tbsp extra virgin olive oil
4 tbsp double cream
**For the garnish**
mint sprigs

**1** Cut away the tough muscle at the side of each scallop and any dark vein, then wash and dry well. Toss with 1 tbsp of the oil, season liberally and then set aside.

**2** To make the broad bean purée, cook the beans in lightly salted boiling water for 3-4 minutes until tender. Drain well and transfer to a blender. Add the remaining ingredients, except the cream, and purée until smooth. Transfer to a small pan, add the cream and warm through. Keep warm.

**3** Heat a ridged griddle or heavy based pan until smoking, add the scallops and cook for 1 minute, then turn and cook the other side for 1 minute. Transfer to a warm plate and rest for a further 1 minute.

**4** For the dressing, mix the remaining 2 tbsp oil with the lemon juice and seasoning. Arrange the scallops on individual plates with the bean purée. Drizzle with the dressing and garnish with mint to serve.

**Note** The bean purée can be prepared ahead. To serve, add the cream and heat through.

A creamy minted bean purée is the perfect partner to sweet, char-griddled scallops.

# Indian spiced monkfish chappatis

2 monkfish fillets, each 225g/8oz, skinned
1 garlic clove, crushed
1 tsp grated fresh root ginger
1 tbsp tandoori spice mix
1 tbsp tomato purée
1 tbsp sunflower oil
1½ tbsp lemon juice
**For the raita**
100g/4oz yogurt
¼ tsp salt
¼ tsp sugar
pinch of cayenne pepper
50g/2oz cucumber, peeled and grated
1 tbsp chopped fresh mint
**To finish**
2 chappatis, cut into triangles
sunflower oil, for shallow frying
lemon wedges and mint leaves, to garnish

**1** Place the monkfish in a dish. In a small bowl, mix together the garlic, ginger, tandoori spice, tomato purée, oil and lemon juice. Add to the monkfish, turn to coat and then leave to marinate in a cool place for at least 1 hour.
**2** Meanwhile, mix together the ingredients for the raita. Set aside.
**3** Preheat the grill. Lay the monkfish on the grill rack and grill for 6-8 minutes, turning halfway, until cooked through. Leave to rest in a warm place for 5 minutes.
**4** Meanwhile, heat a thin layer of oil in a frying pan and fry the chappati triangles for 1 minute until crisp. Drain on kitchen paper.
**5** Slice the monkfish and sandwich between the chappati triangles. Serve garnished with lemon and mint, accompanied by the raita.

Grilled monkfish fillets infused with tandoori spices are served between crisp fried chappatis, with a cooling cucumber raita.

# Prawn wonton soup

1.2 litres/2 pints vegetable stock

4 red chillies, bruised

2 slices fresh root ginger

2 tbsp rice vinegar

2 tbsp light soy sauce

2 tsp sugar

1 tsp sesame oil

**For the wontons**

175g/6oz small raw prawns, peeled

125g/4oz fresh cod fillet, skinned
  and diced

2 spring onions, chopped

1 garlic clove, crushed

grated rind and juice of ½ lime

1 tbsp chopped fresh coriander
  leaves

salt and pepper

20 wonton wrappers

1 small egg, beaten

**For the garnish**

coriander sprigs

**1** Put the stock into a pan with the chillies, ginger, rice vinegar, soy sauce, sugar and sesame oil. Bring to the boil, cover and simmer gently for about 20 minutes.

**2** Devein the prawns, wash and pat dry. Put in a food processor with the cod, spring onions, garlic, lime rind and juice, and the coriander. Purée until fairly smooth, then season with a little salt and pepper.

**3** Brush each wonton wrapper with a little beaten egg and place a spoonful of the prawn mixture in the centre. Draw up the edges over the filling and pinch together at the top to form small parcels.

**4** Drop the wontons into the soup, return to a rolling boil, and then simmer for 3-4 minutes.

**5** Ladle the soup into warmed bowls and serve topped with coriander sprigs.

You can buy the wonton wrappers for this fragrant soup from oriental food stores.

# Garlic prawn and mozzarella salad

20 large raw prawns, peeled
3 tbsp extra virgin olive oil
2 garlic cloves, crushed
1 red chilli, seeded and chopped
225g/8oz buffalo mozzarella cheese,
 sliced
4 ripe plum tomatoes, sliced

**For the basil oil**
15g/½oz fresh basil leaves
4 tbsp extra virgin olive oil
½ tsp lemon juice
salt and pepper
**For the garnish**
basil leaves

**1** Start by making the basil oil. Roughly tear the leaves and place in a blender with the oil, lemon juice and 1½ tsp boiling water. Work until smooth, then transfer to a bowl. Season with salt and pepper to taste.
**2** Devein the prawns, rinse and pat dry with kitchen paper. Heat the oil in a large frying pan. Add the prawns, garlic and chilli. Fry, stirring, over a medium heat for 4-5 minutes until the prawns are cooked through.
**3** Arrange the mozzarella and tomato slices on individual serving plates and top with the hot prawns and their pan juices. Garnish with basil leaves and serve immediately, drizzled with the basil oil.

**Note** Mozzarella made from cow's milk can be used, but authentic buffalo mozzarella lends a superior flavour and texture.

Hot garlic prawns are piled onto sliced tomatoes and buffalo mozzarella, then dressed with an emerald green basil oil.

# Vietnamese tamarind and prawn soup

350g/12oz small raw tiger prawns
900ml/1½ pints vegetable stock
2 lemon grass stalks, roughly chopped
2 slices fresh galangal or root ginger
2 shallots, diced
2 red chillies

50g/2oz flat rice noodles
1 celery stick, sliced
1 tbsp caster sugar
1 tbsp Thai fish sauce
2 tbsp tamarind juice (see note)
1 tbsp each chopped fresh coriander, mint and basil
4 cooked prawns in shells, to garnish

**1** Remove, rinse and reserve the heads and shells from the prawns. Devein the prawns and set aside. Put the prawn shells and heads in a pan with the stock, lemon grass, galangal or ginger, shallots and 1 whole chilli. Bring to the boil, cover and simmer gently for 30 minutes. Strain the flavoured stock into a clean pan.

**2** Put the noodles in a bowl, pour on boiling water and then leave to soak for 5 minutes.

**3** Meanwhile, seed and chop the remaining chilli. Add to the stock with the prawns, celery, sugar, fish sauce and tamarind juice. Simmer gently for 2-3 minutes until the prawns are cooked. Stir in the herbs.

**4** Drain the noodles thoroughly and divide between warm soup bowls. Spoon the soup over the noodles and garnish with the whole prawns to serve.

**Note** Dried tamarind pulp is available from Indian food stores and some supermarkets. To make tamarind juice, dissolve 50g/2oz tamarind pulp in 150ml/¼ pint boiling water, then press through a sieve.

# Smoked salmon parcels

Illustrated on previous pages

450g/1lb sliced smoked salmon
100g/4oz cooked peeled prawns
175g/6oz ricotta cheese
50g/2oz crème fraîche
1 tbsp chopped fresh chervil
1 tbsp chopped fresh chives
1 tbsp lemon juice

salt and pepper
**For the garnish**
salmon caviar
crème fraîche
chervil sprigs
**To serve**
toasted slices of brioche

**1** Line 4 timbales or ramekins with the best smoked salmon slices, using about 300g/10oz; allow sufficient overhang to cover the tops. Roughly chop the remaining smoked salmon.

**2** Put the chopped salmon and prawns in a food processor. Add the ricotta, crème fraîche, herbs, lemon juice, pepper and a little salt; process until fairly smooth.

**3** Spoon the ricotta mixture into the lined timbales or ramekins and spread evenly. Carefully fold the excess smoked salmon over the top to enclose the filling. Wrap the ramekins tightly with cling film and chill in the refrigerator for several hours.

**4** To serve, unmould the salmon mousses onto individual serving plates and garnish with a little extra crème fraîche, salmon caviar and chervil sprigs. Serve with warm toasted brioche.

Jewel-like salmon eggs and crisp, toasted brioche elevate these simple parcels to a decadent starter.

# Scallop, pancetta and mushroom bruschetta

8 large scallops, cleaned
4 thick slices country bread
1 garlic clove, peeled and halved
3-4 tbsp olive oil
50g/2oz cubed pancetta or
  bacon lardons

4 large flat mushrooms, cut
  into wedges
salt and pepper
2 tbsp sherry or balsamic vinegar

**1** Cut away the tough muscle at the side of each scallop and any dark vein, then wash and dry. If the scallops are very large, halve them horizontally.
**2** Grill the bread slices on both sides then rub with the garlic and drizzle with olive oil; keep warm.
**3** Heat 2 tbsp oil in a frying pan, add the pancetta or bacon and fry until beginning to brown. Increase the heat, add the scallops and toss over a high heat for 2 minutes or until just opaque. Lift out with a slotted spoon and set aside.
**4** Add the mushrooms to the pan and fry for 2 minutes until softened, adding a little extra oil if needed.
**5** Return the scallops to the pan and stir over a high heat for a few seconds to warm through. Season well, then pile onto the warm bread. Deglaze the pan with the vinegar and pour the juices over the scallops to serve.

Sautéed scallops, cubes of pancetta and chunky mushrooms piled onto slices of grilled country bread rubbed with garlic and olive oil.

# Mussels with coconut and coriander pesto

32 large fresh mussels in shells
2 tbsp freshly grated Parmesan
   cheese
olive oil, for drizzling
**For the pesto**
25g/1oz fresh coriander leaves

1 small garlic clove, crushed
2 tbsp ground almonds
2 tbsp coconut cream
2 tbsp olive oil
pinch of cayenne pepper
salt and pepper

**1** Scrub the mussels thoroughly in several changes of cold water and pull away any 'beards' that are attached to the shells.

**2** Put the mussels in a large pan, with just the water clinging to the shells after washing. Cover the pan with a tight fitting lid and steam for 4 minutes until the shells have opened. Discard any that remain closed.

**3** Refresh the mussels in cold water, drain well and discard the empty half shells. Invert the mussels in their half shells onto kitchen paper to drain thoroughly.

**4** For the pesto, put all the ingredients in a food processor and work to a rough paste.

**5** Place the mussels, open side up, in a grill pan. Spoon a little pesto on top of each one, then sprinkle with the cheese. Drizzle with a little olive oil and grill for 3-4 minutes until bubbling and golden. Let cool for a minute or so before serving, with warm bread.

**Note** You can use ready-made basil pesto as a tasty, quick alternative to this coconut and coriander pesto.

Mussels on their half shell are topped with a creamy coconut and coriander pesto, then sprinkled with Parmesan and grilled.

# Fish timbales with wasabi dressing

**Serves 6**

250g/9oz skinless halibut or
  cod fillet
2 egg whites
450g/1lb skinless salmon or
  trout fillet
300ml/½ pint double cream, chilled
salt and white pepper

**For the dressing**

6 tsp wasabi paste
6 tsp mirin
4 tbsp rice wine vinegar
175ml/6fl oz sunflower oil

**For the garnish**

225g/8oz young spinach, shredded
oil for deep-frying

**1** Cut the halibut into pieces and mince in a food processor. Add a third of the egg white, a little at a time, mixing well between each addition. Transfer to a bowl. Repeat this process with the salmon, adding all of the remaining egg white. Chill both mixtures for 5 minutes.

**2** Gradually stir a third of the cream into the halibut mixture; add the rest to the salmon, a little at a time. Season both mixtures.

**3** Butter six 150ml/¼ pint timbales, or other ovenproof moulds. Divide half of the salmon mix between them. Cover with the halibut mixture, then top with the remaining salmon, to create layers. Chill for up to 3 hours.

**4** For the dressing, shake the ingredients together in a screw-topped jar to emulsify.

**5** Heat the oil for deep-frying to 180C. Fry the shredded spinach in batches for 15-20 seconds until crisp but still bright green. Drain on kitchen paper.

**6** Remove the timbales from the fridge 15 minutes before cooking. Preheat oven to 180C/fan oven 160C/Gas 4. Stand the moulds in a deep roasting tin and surround with a 3mm/⅛in depth of hot water. Cover with a dampened double layer of greaseproof paper. Bake for 15 minutes or until the tops are firm to the touch. Remove from tin and let stand, covered, for 10-15 minutes.

**7** Unmould the timbales onto kitchen paper, then lift onto serving plates. Top with the deep-fried spinach and drizzle the wasabi dressing around the timbales to serve.

A stylish, special occasion starter.

# Sweetcorn and coconut fritters

85g/3oz plain flour
½ tsp baking powder
1 egg, lightly beaten
2 tbsp coconut cream
1 tbsp light soy sauce
1 tbsp lemon juice
185g can sweetcorn kernels, drained
4 lime leaves, finely shredded
   (see note)

1 tbsp chopped fresh coriander
vegetable oil, for deep frying
**For the dipping sauce**
50g/2oz palm or caster sugar
4 tbsp rice wine vinegar
2 tbsp Thai fish sauce
2 tsp chilli sauce

**1** First make the dipping sauce. Warm the ingredients together in a small pan to dissolve the sugar. Set aside to cool.
**2** Sift the flour and baking powder into a bowl and gradually beat in the egg, coconut cream, soy sauce and lemon juice. Stir in the sweetcorn, lime leaves and coriander.
**3** Heat a 5cm/2in depth of vegetable oil in a wok or deep, wide pan until it registers 180C on a sugar thermometer. Drop in spoonfuls of the batter and fry in batches for 2-3 minutes until crisp and golden.
**4** Drain on kitchen paper and keep warm in a low oven while cooking the rest of the fritters. Serve hot, with the dipping sauce.

**Note** Before shredding lime leaves, remove the thick central vein which is often tough.

These fritters make a delicious starter or snack. Try serving with iceberg lettuce and fresh herbs, such as coriander and basil.
To eat, roll the fritter and a few herb leaves in a lettuce leaf and dip into the sauce.

# Warm artichoke and hazelnut salad

4 large globe artichokes, stalks
  removed
2 tbsp extra virgin olive oil
salt and pepper
175g/6oz French beans, trimmed
**For the dressing**
1 small garlic clove, crushed
4 tbsp hazelnut oil

2 tbsp extra virgin olive oil
1 tbsp white wine vinegar
2 tsp wholegrain mustard
**To serve**
25g/1oz hazelnuts, toasted and
  chopped
pecorino or Parmesan shavings

**1** Put the artichokes in a large pan of cold water and bring to the boil.
Simmer, partially covered, for 20 minutes. Lift out and immediately plunge
into cold water; drain.

**2** Trim away the artichoke leaves to reveal the heart. Using a spoon, scoop
out the prickly choke and discard. Toss the artichoke bases in olive oil and
season well.

**3** Preheat a ridged griddle, or grill. Cook the artichoke hearts for 5 minutes
each side, basting with oil, until tender. Cool slightly.

**4** Meanwhile, whisk together the ingredients for the dressing, season to taste.

**5** Cook the beans in boiling salted water for 3 minutes or until just tender;
drain well.

**6** Lay the artichoke bases on warmed plates and arrange the beans on top.
Scatter over the nuts and cheese shavings. Serve drizzled with the dressing.

Freshly grilled artichoke hearts, topped with
hot green beans and pecorino shavings, and
dressed with a hazelnut vinaigrette.

# Asparagus with quail's eggs and prosciutto

Illustrated on previous pages

350g/12oz thin asparagus spears,
 trimmed
1 tbsp olive oil
salt and pepper
12 quail's eggs
4 slices prosciutto, or Parma ham

2 plum tomatoes, skinned, seeded
 and diced
**For the dressing**
3 tbsp extra virgin olive oil
2 tsp lemon juice
truffle oil, for drizzling (optional)

**1** Peel the asparagus stalks, leaving the tips intact. Preheat a ridged griddle, or grill. Brush the asparagus spears with olive oil and cook, turning, for 3-4 minutes, until tender and charred. Season lightly and set aside until cold.
**2** Cook the quail's eggs in boiling water for 2 minutes; drain and plunge into cold water. Once cool, peel and carefully halve the eggs.
**3** Grill the prosciutto slices until crisp and golden; leave to cool, then break them in half.
**4** For the dressing, whisk together the olive oil, lemon juice, and some salt and pepper.
**5** To serve, arrange the asparagus, quail's eggs and prosciutto slices on 4 large serving plates. Scatter over the diced tomatoes. Spoon over the dressing and add a generous drizzle of truffle oil if using.

Grilling asparagus brings out the full, sweet flavour of this wonderful vegetable. Delicate quail's eggs and crisp grilled pancetta are perfect partners.

# Duck and mango salad with star anise

2 small duck breasts, each about
  125g/4oz
juice of ½ orange
1½ tbsp dark soy sauce
1½ tbsp clear honey
½ tsp ground cinnamon
¼ tsp ground star anise
125g/4oz mangetout
125g/4oz mixed salad leaves

1 small mango, peeled, stoned
  and sliced
1 tbsp sesame seeds, toasted
**For the dressing**
6 tbsp groundnut oil
4 tsp sesame oil
1½ tbsp rice wine vinegar
2 tbsp chopped fresh coriander

**1** Pat the duck breasts dry with kitchen paper, then score the fat. Lay them in a shallow dish. Mix the orange juice, soy, honey and spices together, pour over the duck and leave to marinate for 30 minutes.

**2** Lift the duck breasts onto the grill rack, fat side down, reserving 2 tbsp marinade. Grill for 2 minutes, then turn and grill for a further 5-6 minutes or until the duck is crisp on the outside, but still slightly pink in the centre. Cover loosely with foil and leave to rest in a warm place for 5 minutes.

**3** Meanwhile, blanch the mangetout in lightly salted boiling water for 1 minute. Drain, refresh under cold water and pat dry.

**4** Whisk the dressing ingredients together in a bowl. Toss the salad leaves with a little of the dressing and arrange on plates.

**5** Put the reserved marinade and remaining dressing in a small pan. Bring to the boil; remove from heat.

**6** Thinly slice the duck breasts and arrange on the salad leaves with the mangetout and mango slices. Drizzle over the warm dressing and serve scattered with sesame seeds.

If you cannot buy ground star anise, grind whole ones to a powder in a spice grinder.

# Griddled chicken and fig bruschetta

2 large chicken breast fillets (with skin)

2 tbsp balsamic vinegar

1 tsp clear honey

2 tbsp extra virgin olive oil, plus extra for drizzling

salt and pepper

4 large, firm but ripe figs, halved

4 large slices rustic bread

1 peeled garlic clove, halved

4 slices prosciutto

handful of rocket leaves

**1** Make several slashes through the skin side of each chicken breast. Mix together the balsamic vinegar, honey, oil and seasoning. Set aside half of the mixture; brush the rest over the chicken and figs.

**2** Heat a ridged griddle or heavy based frying pan until smoking. Add the chicken and fry for 4-5 minutes each side until charred on the outside and cooked through. Lift out and leave to rest for 5 minutes. Add the figs to the pan and cook for 1-2 minutes until softened.

**3** Meanwhile, lightly toast the bread on both sides under the grill, then rub all over with garlic and drizzle with olive oil; keep warm. Grill the prosciutto for about 1 minute each side until crisp.

**4** Slice the chicken and arrange on the bruschetta with figs, prosciutto and rocket leaves. Season and drizzle over the remaining balsamic sauce to serve.

Ridged griddle pans give food an authentic char-grill flavour. Here, chicken and figs are bathed in a sweetened balsamic sauce, then griddled until charred and tender.

# smart
# pasta

# Pasta with gorgonzola, walnut and herb sauce

2 slices wholemeal bread, crusts
  removed
200ml/7fl oz milk
225g/8oz walnut pieces
1 garlic clove, crushed
125g/4½oz gorgonzola cheese,
  in pieces

4 tbsp extra virgin olive oil
100ml/3½fl oz crème fraîche
6 tbsp chopped fresh parsley
salt and pepper
450g/1lb dried ribbon pasta,
  such as pappardelle, tagliatelle,
  or fettuccine

**1** Preheat oven to 190C/fan oven 170C/Gas 5. Soak the bread in the milk for 10 minutes or until all the milk is absorbed.

**2** Spread the walnuts on a baking sheet and toast in the oven for 5 minutes. Transfer to a plate and allow to cool.

**3** Put the soaked bread, walnuts, garlic, gorgonzola and olive oil in a food processor and work until almost smooth.

**4** Transfer to a bowl and stir in the crème fraîche and chopped parsley. Season generously with pepper, and a little salt if required.

**5** Bring a large pan of salted water to the boil. Add the pasta and cook until al dente. Drain, keeping back 2 tbsp water in the pan. Immediately toss the pasta with the sauce. Cover with a lid and then leave to stand for 3 minutes before serving.

This creamy sauce relies on the heat of the cooked pasta to melt the cheese and warm the ingredients. The flavours develop on standing.

# Walnut and mixed olive spaghetti

**Serves 4-6**

230g jar mixed olives in extra virgin olive oil
75g/2½oz walnuts (ideally freshly shelled)
juice of ½ orange (3-4 tbsp)

500g/1lb 2oz dried wholewheat spaghetti
salt and pepper (black or five pepper mix)
freshly grated Parmesan cheese, to serve

**1** Strain the olives and reserve the oil. Stone and slice the olives. Grate the walnuts, using a mouli grater or food processor.
**2** For the dressing, mix together the orange juice and olive oil.
**3** Cook the spaghetti in a large pan of boiling salted water until al dente. Return to the warm pan and add the olive slices, grated walnuts, dressing and seasoning; toss lightly together. Serve at once, with grated Parmesan and a salad.

Olives give this sauce such a superb flavour that stoning them is worth the effort.

# Fusilli lunghi, peppers and anchovy olives

3 tbsp olive oil
1 large onion, thinly sliced
3 garlic cloves, thinly sliced
2 red peppers, cored, seeded and
 sliced
3 courgettes, cut into sticks
two 400g cans peeled tomatoes in
 rich juice
2 tbsp chopped fresh basil
salt and pepper

300g/10oz dried fusilli lunghi,
 or lasagnette
100g/4oz anchovy stuffed olives,
 halved
**For the topping**
250g tub mascarpone cheese
50g/2oz Parmesan cheese, coarsely
 grated
25g/1oz pine nuts
basil leaves, to garnish

**1** Heat the oil in a large frying pan and fry the onion until golden. Add the garlic, peppers and courgettes, and stir-fry over a high heat for 5 minutes.
**2** Stir in the tomatoes with their juice and the chopped basil. Season and simmer gently for 10 minutes until the vegetables are tender.
**3** Meanwhile, cook the pasta in a large pan of boiling salted water until al dente. Drain the pasta and refresh under cold running water; drain again.
**4** Stir the pasta into the tomato mixture with the olives. Turn into a large ovenproof dish and top with mascarpone. Sprinkle with the Parmesan cheese and pine nuts. (If preparing ahead, cover with cling film and chill.)
**5** To serve, preheat the oven to 200C/fan oven 180C/Gas 6. Bake the pasta dish for 30 minutes or until bubbling. Let stand for a few minutes, then scatter with basil leaves and serve with crusty bread.

**Note** For a vegetarian dish use pimento rather than anchovy stuffed olives.

Anchovy olives provide a piquant flavour, while mascarpone and Parmesan melt to an irresistible creamy topping.

# Pappardelle with sun-dried tomato sauce

Illustrated on previous pages

**Serves 4-6**

50g/2oz sun-dried aubergines
  (see note)
3 garlic cloves, peeled
4 tbsp sun-dried tomato paste
250g/9oz grilled artichoke hearts in
  olive oil (see note)

salt and pepper
500g/1lb 2oz dried pappardelle
4 tbsp roughly torn fresh parsley
50g/2oz pine nuts, toasted

**1** Simmer the sun-dried aubergines in water to cover for 2 minutes. Drain and refresh in cold water; drain and dry on kitchen paper. Cut each slice into 3 long strips.

**2** Simmer the garlic in water to cover for 7-8 minutes until softened. Drain and crush the garlic with the back of a knife, then mix with the sun-dried tomato paste.

**3** Drain the artichoke hearts, reserving 4 tbsp oil; halve any larger ones. Heat the reserved oil in a large frying pan and stir-fry the aubergine until tender. Add the artichokes and heat through. Add the garlic mixture and season; keep warm.

**4** Cook the pasta in a large pan of boiling salted water until al dente. Add 4 tbsp of the cooking liquid to the sauce. Drain the pasta and toss with the hot sauce, parsley and pine nuts to serve.

**Note** Packs of char grilled sun-dried aubergines and jars of grilled artichoke hearts in oil are sold in major supermarkets. Alternatively, substitute 1 large fresh aubergine, thinly sliced, and a jar of artichoke hearts in oil, drained. Brush the aubergine slices with oil and grill on both sides until charred. Fry the artichokes in 2 tbsp olive oil until tinged brown. Add both to the sauce.

Make this delicious sauce in advance and reheat while the pasta is cooking.

# Tortelloni with creamy dolcelatte sauce

500g/1lb 2oz dried tortelloni
salt and pepper
50g/2oz butter
140g/5oz dolcelatte cheese, cut into
  small cubes

175ml/6fl oz double cream
85g/3oz Parmesan cheese, finely
  grated
chopped flat-leaf parsley, to garnish

**1** Cook the tortelloni according to packet instructions or until al dente.
**2** Meanwhile, melt the butter in a small, heavy-based pan over a low heat.
Add the dolcelatte and stir until completely melted. Add the cream and
slowly bring to a simmer, stirring. When the sauce is thick enough to coat
the spoon, stir in the Parmesan. Season to taste.
**3** Drain the tortelloni and toss with the sauce. Serve sprinkled with chopped
parsley and accompanied by a salad.

This is excellent with any bought tortelloni.
The dolcelatte must be young, not aged.

# Herb and parmesan pasta

**Serves 4-6**

190g/6½oz type '00' pasta flour

20g/¾oz Parmesan cheese,
  finely grated

2 medium eggs (preferably organic,
  for yolk colour)

48 flat leaf parsley leaves,
  stalks removed

salt

2 tbsp oil, for cooking

**1** To make the pasta, put all the ingredients in a food processor and pulse until the mixture forms lumpy grains. Tip onto a lightly floured surface (not marble) and knead together until smooth. Wrap in cling film and refrigerate for at least 3 hours.

**2** Cut the pasta into manageable portions; keep wrapped. Roll out, one piece at a time, using a pasta machine. Pass dough through the widest setting at least 3 times, then gradually narrow the setting as you roll out, until you have a thin pliable sheet of pasta.

**3** Lay parsley leaves on one pasta sheet at 2.5cm/1in intervals and then place another sheet of pasta on top to sandwich the leaves. Roll through the machine on a medium setting, then once through on a narrow setting. Cut into rectangles around the leaves, with a pasta wheel or a knife. Leave to dry slightly on greaseproof paper for 3 hours (or overnight).

**4** Add the pasta to a large pan of boiling salted water with 2 tbsp oil and cook for 3-4 minutes until al dente. Serve with your favourite pasta sauce.

Parsley leaves are sandwiched between layers of homemade pasta to stunning effect. A fresh tomato sauce is the ideal complement.

# Pasta with red pepper and rocket sauce

**Serves 4-6**

1 quantity Herb and parmesan pasta
  (page 49), or 500g/1lb 2oz dried
  pappardelle

**For the sauce**

8 tbsp extra virgin olive oil

2 onions, finely chopped

4 red peppers, halved, cored
  and seeded

salt and pepper

**To finish**

3 tbsp oil

100g/4oz rocket leaves

**1** To make the sauce, heat 4 tbsp of the oil in a heavy-based frying pan and gently fry the onions over a low heat for 10 minutes, turning occasionally. Grill the peppers until charred, let cool slightly, then skin. Dice the pepper flesh and add to the onions with the remaining oil. Cook on a low heat for 20 minutes until soft, but not brown.

**2** Add the pasta to a large pan of boiling salted water with 2 tbsp oil and cook until al dente: allow 3-4 minutes for fresh pasta; longer for dried pasta (refer to packet instructions). Meanwhile, heat 1 tbsp oil in a large pan, add the rocket and cook briefly until just wilted. Drain the pasta and serve at once on the wilted rocket, topped with the hot sauce.

Parsley leaves are sandwiched between layers of homemade pasta and served in a vivid pepper sauce with rocket.

# Pasta with roast peppers and shallots

2 red peppers
8 shallots, thickly sliced
4 tbsp olive oil
450g/1lb dried chunky pasta shapes,
 such as rigatoni or shells

salt and pepper
2 tbsp balsamic vinegar
freshly grated Parmesan cheese,
 to serve

**1** Preheat oven to 200C/fan oven 180C/ Gas 6. Place the whole red peppers and sliced shallots in a small roasting tin and drizzle with the oil. Turn the peppers and shallots to coat with the oil.
**2** Roast in the oven for 10-15 minutes until the shallots are golden brown. Using a slotted spoon, transfer the shallots to a saucepan.
**3** Roast the peppers, turning occasionally, for a further 15-20 minutes until charred. Leave until cool enough to handle, then skin. Halve the peppers, discard the seeds and cut the flesh into strips. Add the pepper strips and any juices to the shallots.
**4** Bring a large pan of salted water to the boil. Add the pasta and cook until al dente.
**5** Meanwhile, reheat the shallot mixture and stir in the balsamic vinegar. Cook over a high heat for 1 minute. Season with salt and pepper to taste.
**6** Drain the pasta, keeping back 2 tbsp water in the pan. Immediately toss with the sauce. Serve accompanied by freshly grated Parmesan.

For a treat, serve topped with a dollop of creamy mascarpone flavoured with cracked black peppercorns.

# Lemon pasta salad with mushrooms

Illustrated on previous pages

**Serves 3-4; or 6 as part of a meal**
1 tbsp olive oil
350g/12oz flat mushrooms,
   cut into wedges
1 tsp coriander seeds, crushed
2 tsp finely chopped fresh sage

½ tsp grated lemon zest
3 tbsp lemon juice
250g/9oz fresh ballerine, or
   farfalle pasta
salt and pepper
sage leaves, to garnish

**1** Heat the oil in a frying pan and stir-fry the mushrooms for 2-3 minutes, then add the coriander and sage. Cook for 2-3 minutes until the mushroom juices start to run. Remove from the heat and add the lemon zest and juice.
**2** Add the pasta to a large pan of boiling salted water and cook for a few minutes only, until al dente. Drain, refresh in cold water and drain well.
**3** Toss the warm mushrooms and pasta together. Season with salt and pepper to taste. Serve garnished with sage.

**Variation** Replace the mushrooms with 3 red or orange peppers, skinned, seeded and sliced.

This tangy pasta salad is best served freshly made, while it is still warm.

# Pasta salad with olives, peppers and artichokes

2 large red or orange peppers
2 garlic cloves, peeled
175g/6oz dried pasta shapes, such as spirals or shells
180g tub marinated grilled artichoke hearts in olive oil (see note)
40g/1½oz pitted black olives

1 tbsp capers, drained
2 tbsp chopped fresh flat leaf parsley
**For the dressing**
1 tbsp balsamic vinegar
3 tbsp extra virgin olive oil
salt and pepper

**1** Put the peppers, skin-side up, on the grill rack with the unpeeled garlic cloves (for the dressing). Grill under a medium-high heat, turning from time to time, until the pepper skins are blistered and charred. Set aside the garlic for the dressing. Put the grilled peppers in a bowl, cover tightly with cling film and leave to cool slightly.

**2** Peel away the skins from the peppers, then halve, core and remove the seeds, reserving the juices. Cut the peppers into strips.

**3** For the dressing, squeeze the garlic flesh from the skins into a bowl and add the balsamic vinegar and olive oil. Whisk to combine and season with salt and pepper.

**4** Cook the pasta in a large pan of boiling salted water until al dente. Drain, then refresh under cold running water and drain thoroughly. Tip the pasta into a large bowl, add the dressing and toss to mix.

**5** Drain and slice the artichoke hearts. Add to the pasta with the grilled pepper strips, olives and capers. Cover and leave to stand at room temperature for an hour or so before serving, to allow the flavours to develop.

**6** Add the parsley to the salad and check the seasoning before serving.

**Note** If you cannot buy grilled artichoke hearts, use a jar of artichoke hearts in olive oil instead.

# Saffron pasta

**Makes 350g/12oz**
¼ tsp saffron strands
2 eggs (preferably organic,
    for yolk colour)
200g/7oz type '00' pasta flour
extra flour, for dusting

**1** Crush the saffron strands, using a mortar and pestle, add the eggs and
then mix well.
**2** Put the egg mixture into a food processor, add the flour and pulse until
the mixture forms lumpy grains.
**3** Turn onto a lightly floured surface (not marble, as this is too cold), and
knead until smooth. Wrap in cling film and leave to rest in the refrigerator
for at least 3 hours.
**4** Use a pasta machine to roll the dough into thin sheets to make ravioli;
for tagliatelle or spaghetti, fit the appropriate cutters to the machine after
rolling. Cook in boiling salted water until al dente, allowing 3-4 minutes for
ribbon pasta; 4-6 minutes for ravioli. Serve with your favourite sauce.

### Variations
**Sun-dried tomato pasta** Replace the saffron with 25g/1oz chopped sun-dried
tomatoes (not in oil). Process to a purée with the eggs.
**Mushroom pasta** Replace the saffron with 20g/¾oz dried porcini, ground
to a powder.
**Spinach pasta** Wilt 125g spinach in 1 tbsp oil, drain well and squeeze out
all moisture. Purée in the processor with the eggs.

**Note** For convenience, you can make the pasta 1-2 days in advance. Keep
tightly wrapped in cling film, in the fridge, until required. If you are
making ravioli, prepare these a day ahead, freeze overnight and cook from
frozen. (They are best frozen for a short time only).

Satisfying to prepare – and not too difficult –
homemade pasta is well worth the effort.

# Saffron ravioli with butternut squash

Also illustrated on following pages

750g/1lb 10oz butternut squash
4 tbsp sunflower oil
salt and pepper
60g/2¼oz pecorino or Parmesan
cheese, grated
1 quantity Saffron pasta dough
(page 58)
1 egg white

**For the dressing**
4 garlic cloves, thinly sliced
150ml/¼ pint extra virgin olive oil
85g/3oz black olives, stoned and
sliced
4 tsp fresh thyme leaves, roughly
chopped
85g/3oz pecorino or Parmesan cheese

**1** Preheat oven to 200C/fan oven 180C/Gas 6. Quarter the squash, put on a
baking sheet and drizzle with oil; season. Roast for 55 minutes until very soft.
Discard seeds. Purée the squash, cheese and ¼ tsp pepper in a food processor.
**2** Cut the pasta into manageable portions; keep wrapped. Roll out, one piece
at a time, using a pasta machine. Pass dough through the widest setting at
least 3 times, then gradually narrow the setting until you have a thin pliable
sheet. Pass through thinnest setting 3 times. Repeat with remaining dough.
**3** Place a pasta sheet on a board and stamp out discs, with a 6cm/2½in fluted
cutter. Lay half the discs on a sheet of cling film and paint the edges with
egg white. Put a teaspoon of squash filling in the centre of each and top
with the other discs, sticking the edges together without squashing the filling.
**4** Repeat with the rest of the pasta to make about 35 ravioli. Place on trays
lined with cling film, spacing apart. Freeze or use within 1 hour.
**5** For the dressing, warm the garlic and oil in a small pan until the garlic
begins to turn golden. Add the olives, thyme and pepper. Set aside to infuse.
**6** When ready to serve, bring a large pan of salted water to the boil and add
2 tbsp oil. Cook the ravioli for 4-6 minutes until al dente; drain. Serve with
the warm dressing poured over, and topped with pecorino shavings.

Homemade ravioli served with a warm
dressing of garlic, olives and thyme.

# Fettuccine with asparagus and pancetta

¼ tsp saffron threads
140g/5oz pancetta, diced
450g/1lb asparagus
450g/1lb dried spinach fettuccine
salt and pepper
85g/3oz butter

4 spring onions, thinly sliced
125ml/4fl oz dry white wine
250ml/8fl oz double cream
3 tbsp snipped fresh chives
50g/2oz Parmesan cheese, finely
  grated

**1** Soak the saffron threads in 2 tbsp hot water.
**2** Preheat a heavy-based frying pan, then add the pancetta and fry, stirring, until golden and crisp. Set aside.
**3** Cut the asparagus into short lengths, keeping the tips whole. Add to a pan of boiling salted water and par-boil for 3-4 minutes; drain.
**4** Cook the fettuccine in a large pan of boiling salted water until al dente.
**5** Meanwhile, melt the butter in a large frying pan. Add the spring onions and cook for 1 minute, then add the asparagus and sauté for 1-2 minutes. Pour in the wine and cook for 3 minutes. Stir in the cream, saffron and soaking liquid. Bring to a simmer.
**6** Drain the pasta and add to the saffron sauce with the chives, Parmesan and pancetta. Toss well, season and serve.

Spinach flavoured tagliatelle tossed in a creamy saffron sauce with fresh asparagus, spring onions, pancetta and chives.

# Seafood spaghetti

**Serves 4-6**

1kg/2lb 4oz mussels in shells,
  cleaned
250g/9oz peeled, raw tiger prawns
25g/1oz butter
100ml/3½fl oz white wine
1 tsp finely grated lemon zest

2 tsp mild curry paste
300ml/½ pint single cream
175g/6oz smoked salmon
  trimmings, sliced
salt and pepper
500g/1lb 2oz dried spaghetti
lemon wedges, to serve

**1** Discard any damaged mussels or any open ones that do not close when tapped sharply. Halve the prawns lengthwise and devein.

**2** Melt the butter in a large pan with the wine and 4 tbsp water. Add the mussels, cover tightly and cook briskly for 4 minutes, or until the shells open, shaking the pan from time to time. Discard any mussels which have not opened.

**3** Lift out the mussels with a slotted spoon and set aside 12 for the garnish. Remove the rest of the mussels from their shells.

**4** Add the prawns to the pan. Cook, stirring, for 4-5 minutes until they turn pink. Stir in the lemon zest, curry paste and cream, then add the smoked salmon and shelled mussels. Heat through gently and season with salt and pepper to taste.

**5** Meanwhile, cook the spaghetti in a large pan of boiling salted water until al dente. Drain and toss with the seafood sauce. Serve immediately, garnished with the reserved mussels and accompanied by lemon wedges.

**Note** Always add pasta to a large saucepan containing plenty of boiling water. Cook at a fast boil to prevent sticking.

Serve this luxurious pasta dish with a leafy green salad, dressed with lemon juice and light olive oil.

# Seafood pasta with a coconut cream sauce

100ml/3½fl oz double cream
100ml/3½fl oz coconut milk
1-2 tbsp sun-dried tomato paste
450g/1lb dried spinach tagliatelle, smoked salmon tagliatelle, or egg pappardelle
salt and pepper
1 tbsp olive oil
3 spring onions, thinly sliced
1 garlic clove, crushed
1 tsp grated fresh root ginger
1 red chilli, seeded and finely chopped
300g/10oz cooked peeled tiger prawns
200g/7oz white crabmeat
3 tbsp chopped fresh coriander leaves
coriander leaves, to garnish

**1** In a bowl, whisk together the cream, coconut milk and sun-dried tomato paste; set aside.
**2** Cook the pasta in a large pan of boiling salted water until al dente.
**3** Meanwhile, heat the oil in a large pan. Add the spring onions, garlic, ginger and chilli. Stir-fry for 2 minutes, then add the prawns and crabmeat. Heat through, stirring, for 1 minute.
**4** Add the cream mixture and slowly bring to a simmer, stirring. Add the chopped coriander, stir well and season with salt and pepper to taste.
**5** Drain the pasta and toss with the seafood sauce. Serve immediately, scattered with coriander leaves.

A delicious fusion of prawns and crabmeat, flavoured with spring onions, chilli and coriander in a coconut cream sauce.

# Squid ink pasta with a spicy seafood sauce

3 tbsp extra virgin olive oil
4 garlic cloves, finely chopped
450g/1lb dried squid ink pasta
salt and pepper
300g/10oz cleaned baby squid, cut
  into rings
300g/10oz raw tiger prawns, peeled
  and deveined

1-2 red chillies, seeded and finely
  sliced
150ml/¼ pint dry white wine
400g can chopped tomatoes
3 tbsp chopped flat-leaf parsley
flat leaf parsley sprigs, to garnish

**1** Heat the oil in a large, heavy-based frying pan and gently sauté the garlic until softened.

**2** Meanwhile, cook the pasta in a large pan of boiling salted water until al dente.

**3** Add the squid and prawns to the garlic. Stir-fry over a high heat for 2-3 minutes, then add the chilli and wine. Lower heat to medium and cook for 3-4 minutes. Add the tomatoes and parsley and cook for a further 3-4 minutes. Season to taste.

**4** Drain the pasta, toss with the seafood sauce and then serve, garnished with flat leaf parsley.

Squid, tiger prawns, chilli, tomatoes, wine and a hint of garlic are a combined with black squid ink pasta for a dramatic dish.

# Individual salmon lasagne

Illustrated on previous pages

850ml/1½ pints milk
85g/3oz butter
85g/3oz plain flour
1 fresh bay leaf
salt and pepper
2 tbsp creamed horseradish
squeeze of lemon juice (optional)

500g/1lb 2oz boneless skinless
   salmon fillets, cut into small cubes
8 sheets dried (no-need to pre-cook)
   lasagne
6 smoked salmon slices
**For the topping**
85g/3oz Emmental cheese, grated

**1** Pour the milk into a pan. Add the butter, flour, bay leaf and seasoning. Whisk over a medium heat, until the sauce is smooth and thickened.

**2** Pour half the sauce into a bowl and add the horseradish with a squeeze of lemon juice to taste. Stir in the fresh salmon cubes; set aside. Leave the bay leaf in the remaining sauce, to infuse.

**3** Par-cook the lasagne in a large pan of boiling salted water with 2 tbsp oil added for 5 minutes (to shorten the baking time).

**4** Spoon a third of the salmon mixture into four individual pie dishes, cover with a sheet of lasagne, then spoon over the rest of the mixture.

**5** Cover with the remaining lasagne sheets and top with a slice of smoked salmon. Discard the bay leaf, then spoon the sauce over the smoked salmon.

**6** Halve the other 2 smoked salmon slices and place one on each portion. Top with the cheese. (If preparing ahead, cover and chill for up to 24 hours.)

**7** To serve, preheat oven to 190C/fan oven 170C/Gas 5. Bake the lasagne for 30 minutes until bubbling. If necessary, brown under the grill. Serve with a fennel, baby spinach and orange salad.

Creamed horseradish marries this flavour combination of fresh and smoked salmon perfectly. Avoid overcooking the lasagne.

# Plaice and caper stuffed conchiglioni

250g/9oz dried conchiglioni
  (about 40 very large, unbroken
  pasta shells)
salt and pepper
500g/1lb 2oz plaice fillet, skinned

425ml/¾ pint vegetable stock
1 large or 2 small fennel bulbs,
  thinly sliced
1 tbsp capers, rinsed
25g/1oz butter, chilled

**1** Preheat oven to 180C/fan oven 160C/Gas 4. Cook the pasta shells in a large pan of boiling salted water until al dente. Drain and immediately rinse in cold water; drain.
**2** Heat the stock in a pan, add the fennel and poach for 15 minutes until tender. Drain and spread in a shallow ovenproof dish.
**3** Cut the plaice into about 40 pieces and pop one piece into each pasta shell. Place the shells, stuffed side up, on top of the fennel. Sprinkle with the capers and season generously with pepper. Place a tiny dot of butter in each shell.
**4** Cover the dish with foil and bake for 30 minutes or until the fish is opaque.

**Variation** Bake the stuffed pasta shells on a bed of thinly sliced fresh tomatoes instead of poached fennel. You will need 4 large tomatoes.

Chunks of fish nestling in large pasta shells on a bed of sweet, poached fennel. Assemble 1-2 hours in advance and bake as required.

# Corn spaghetti with squid and salmon

**Serves 6**

7.5cm/3in piece fresh root ginger,
  peeled
oil for deep-frying
650g/1lb 7oz salmon fillet, skinned
  and cut into 2.5cm/1in pieces
2 tbsp olive oil
salt and pepper
350g/12oz baby squid, cleaned and
  cut into 1cm/½in pieces
500g/1lb 2oz dried corn spaghetti

**For the dressing**

150ml/¼ pint olive oil
3 tbsp dry white wine
2 tbsp lemon juice
2 tbsp chopped fresh dill

**For the garnish**

dill sprigs

**1** Finely slice the ginger lengthways, then cut into fine julienne. Heat a
5cm/2in depth of oil in a deep pan to 170C. Deep-fry the ginger until golden.
Drain on kitchen paper.

**2** Toss the salmon in 1 tbsp oil and season well. Repeat with the squid.
Preheat oven to 150C/fan oven 130C/Gas 2.

**3** Heat a non-stick frying pan until very hot. Add the salmon and sear for
30 seconds each side. Remove and keep warm in a covered dish in the oven.
Repeat with squid.

**4** Add the spaghetti to a large pan of boiling salted water and cook until
al dente.

**5** Meanwhile, whisk the dressing ingredients together, except the dill, in
a pan; warm through.

**6** Drain the pasta well and place in a bowl. Add the chopped dill and
dressing; toss well. Fold in the salmon and squid.

**7** Top with dill sprigs, a generous grinding of pepper, and the ginger
julienne to serve.

Corn pasta has a wonderful colour and looks
great with pink salmon.

# All-in-one curried noodles

175g/6oz rice stick or egg thread
  noodles
1 tbsp sunflower oil
1 red pepper, cored, seeded and cut
  into thin sticks
1 red onion, cut into wedges
100g/4oz baby corn cobs, halved
  lengthways
100g/4oz sugar snaps, halved
100g/4oz close cup mushrooms,
  halved

2 tbsp madras curry paste
400g can coconut milk
2 tbsp light soy sauce
200g/7oz extra large cooked
  tiger prawns (thawed and dried
  if frozen)
4 tbsp chopped fresh coriander
coriander sprigs, to garnish

**1** Put the noodles in a bowl, pour on boiling water and leave to soak for
5 minutes or according to packet directions.
**2** Heat the oil in a large pan or wok. Add the red pepper and onion and
stir-fry for a few minutes until starting to soften.
**3** Toss in the baby corn and stir-fry for 2 minutes, then add the sugar snaps
and mushrooms, and stir-fry for a further few minutes.
**4** Stir in the curry paste, then pour in the coconut milk and soy sauce. Add
the prawns and chopped coriander; toss well. Divide the noodles between
warmed bowls, add the curried sauce and serve garnished with coriander.

**Note** Baby corn cobs and sugar snaps are available in 200g/7oz mixed
packets from some supermarkets.

Tiger prawns tossed with noodles and plenty
of vegetables in a curried coconut sauce.

# Penne with meatballs in tomato sauce

**For the meatballs**
450g/1lb lean beef mince
grated zest of ½ lemon
1 tsp ground coriander
½ tsp ground cumin
2 tbsp chopped fresh oregano
1 tbsp chopped fresh coriander
  or parsley
1 tbsp harissa paste
25g/1oz fresh white breadcrumbs

1 small egg, beaten
salt and pepper
1 tbsp olive oil
**For the sauce and pasta**
1 shallot, finely chopped
1 garlic clove, crushed
400g carton passata
500g/1lb 2oz dried penne, or spirals
2 tbsp chopped fresh parsley

**1** To prepare the meatballs, put the beef mince in a bowl with the lemon zest, spices, herbs, harissa paste and breadcrumbs. Season generously with salt and pepper and mix, using your hands until evenly blended. Work in enough beaten egg to bind the mixture, then shape into about 30 small balls.
**2** Heat the olive oil in a large frying pan, add the meatballs and fry over medium heat, turning to brown evenly, for about 5 minutes. Remove with a slotted spoon and drain off all but 1 tbsp fat from the pan.
**3** Add the shallots and garlic to the pan and fry gently for about 5 minutes until beginning to soften. Add the passata and bring to a simmer, then season well with salt and pepper. Return the meatballs to the pan and simmer, partially covered, for 15 minutes or until cooked through.
**4** In the meantime, cook the pasta in a large pan of boiling salted water until al dente. Drain and return to the pan. Add 3-4 tbsp of the sauce from the meatballs and toss to mix.
**5** Divide the pasta among warmed plates, top with the meatballs in tomato sauce and scatter with the chopped parsley to serve.

Flavoured with oregano, harissa, cumin and coriander, these tasty meatballs are delicious served with pasta and a simple tomato sauce.

# Caserecce gratin with taleggio and prosciutto

**Serves 6**
425ml/¾ pint milk
25g/1oz plain flour
25g/1oz butter
salt and pepper
freshly grated nutmeg
2 tbsp sunflower oil

350g/12oz young leaf spinach
500g/1lb 2oz dried caserecce, or
   spirals
140g/5oz prosciutto, cut into strips
250g/9oz taleggio cheese, finely
   diced

**1** Preheat oven to 200C/fan oven 180C/Gas 6. Grease a 20 x 25cm/10 x 8in gratin dish.
**2** Place the milk, flour and butter in a heavy-based pan over a medium heat and whisk until thick. Season with pepper, nutmeg and a little salt.
**3** Heat the oil in a large wok or pan, add the spinach and cook over a high heat for 1 minute only, turning continuously. Tip into a colander and drain.
**4** Add the pasta to a large pan of boiling salted water. Cook for 2 minutes less than the suggested time on the packet. Drain well and tip into the gratin dish.
**5** Add the spinach, prosciutto, two thirds of the cheese, and the sauce. Season with pepper. Toss well. Dot the surface with the remaining cheese and dust with nutmeg.
**6** Cover with foil and bake for 10 minutes. Uncover and bake for a further 5 minutes.

**Note** For convenience, make in advance. Keep covered in the fridge but bring to room temperature before baking, allowing an extra 10 minutes in the oven.

A slightly twisted pasta, caserecce is ideal for gratins. Taleggio has a delicious tang, though gruyère may be used.

# smart
# fish

# Prawns on crackling rice pancakes

250g packet instant risotto, preferably saffron flavoured
1 garlic clove, finely chopped
1cm/¾in piece fresh root ginger, peeled and grated
2 tbsp chopped fresh chives
4 spring onions, finely chopped
salt and pepper
750g/1lb 10oz medium raw prawns in shells
25g/1oz butter
2 tbsp sunflower oil
2 tbsp Thai red curry paste
chives, to garnish

**1** To make the risotto, cook the rice according to the packet instructions, together with the garlic, ginger, chives, spring onions and seasoning. Tip onto a tray; allow to cool. When cold, shape into 8 cakes, with wet hands.
**2** Shell the prawns, leaving the tail shells on.
**3** Melt the butter in a frying pan and cook the pancakes carefully, a few at a time, until golden and crispy on one side; turn and cook the other side. Avoid moving during cooking or they might break up. Keep warm.
**4** Heat the oil in a wok or frying pan, add the curry paste and cook, stirring, for 1 minute. Add the prawns and stir-fry for 3-4 minutes until cooked. Serve at once, on the rice cakes. Garnish with chives.

**Note** Instant '12 minute' risotto rice (eg. Riso Gallo) is available from most supermarkets.

An impressive dish to rustle up from the storecupboard, using instant risotto rice.

# Deep-fried prawns with harissa salsa

**Serves 3-4**

24 large raw prawns

400ml/14fl oz well seasoned fish
   stock

pinch each of turmeric and
   chilli powder

225g/8oz couscous

8 tbsp chopped fresh coriander leaves

2 red chillies, seeded and finely diced

salt and pepper

oil for deep-frying

seasoned flour, for coating

2 eggs, beaten

**For the harissa salsa**

2 garlic cloves, crushed

1 tsp ground coriander

2 tsp ground caraway seeds

2 tsp mild chilli powder
   (preferably ancho)

1 tsp sugar

1 tomato, seeded and finely diced

50ml/2fl oz olive oil

juice of 1 lemon

**For the garnish**

deep-fried flat leaf parsley

**1** Shell and devein the prawns, leaving the tail shells on; set aside.

**2** Next, prepare the harissa salsa. Mash the garlic with the spices and a little salt, stir in the remaining ingredients and set aside.

**3** For the prawn coating, bring the stock to the boil, and add the turmeric and chilli powder. Pour over the couscous, cover and leave until the liquid is absorbed. When cool enough to handle, break up the couscous. Add the coriander and chillies; season well.

**4** Heat oil for deep-frying to 160C. Dip the prawns into seasoned flour, then egg, then coat with couscous. Deep-fry, a few at a time, for 3-4 minutes until cooked; drain on kitchen paper. Serve garnished with fried parsley and accompanied by the harissa salsa.

Serve these spicy couscous coated prawns as a light lunch or fish course.

# Seafood with pine nuts and garlic

**Serves 4-6**

40g/1½oz raisins
50ml/2fl oz brandy
3 garlic cloves, crushed
85g/3oz pine nuts, lightly toasted
salt and pepper
6 tbsp olive oil
1 large onion, finely chopped
8 tomatoes, skinned and chopped

2 tsp paprika
4 fresh bay leaves
125ml/4fl oz dry white wine
30 mussels in shells, cleaned
24 clams in shells, cleaned (optional)
8-12 whole large raw prawns
700g/1lb 9oz thick cod fillet, cut into
    5cm/2in chunks
8-12 small new potatoes, cooked

**1** Soak the raisins in the brandy for 1 hour. Mash the garlic and two thirds of the pine nuts to a paste with a little salt.

**2** Heat 3 tbsp oil in a heavy-based pan and gently fry the onion until soft. Increase the heat and add the tomatoes, paprika, bay leaves, seasoning and wine. Stir well until beginning to thicken. Transfer to a bowl.

**3** Bring 400ml/14 fl oz salted water to the boil in a large pan. Add mussels, and clams if using. Cover and shake the pan over a medium heat for about 4 minutes, until the shells open. Drain, reserving the liquor; discard any unopened ones. Strain the liquor; stir a little into the garlic paste.

**4** Heat the remaining oil in a deep pan and sauté the prawns for 1 minute. Add the raisins and brandy and cook for 1 minute. Stir in the tomato mix.

**5** Add the remaining liquor to the pan and bring to a gentle simmer, then remove the prawns with a slotted spoon. Add the cod to the pan and cook for 5 minutes; remove. Increase the heat, then add the garlic paste and potatoes. Simmer for a few minutes.

**6** To serve, add all of the seafood to the pan and heat through gently. Sprinkle with the remaining pine nuts.

This rich Spanish stew is substantial enough to serve as a meal in itself. Accompany with plenty of flat bread to mop up the tasty juices.

# Salmon with anchovies and capers

**Serves 4-6**

1.5-1.6kg/3¼-3½lb whole salmon,
  cleaned
8 anchovy fillets
1 tbsp capers

small handful of fresh parsley
  sprigs, stems removed
1 tsp grated lemon rind
juice of ½ lemon
pepper

**1** Preheat oven to 220C/fan oven 200C/Gas 7. Make 4 or 5 diagonal slits in the skin on each side of the salmon.

**2** Finely chop the anchovy fillets, capers and fresh parsley. Mix together with the grated lemon rind and the lemon juice.

**3** Press this paste into the cuts in the fish. Season the fish with pepper, wrap in oiled foil and seal loosely. Bake for 45 minutes.

**4** Leave the salmon, still wrapped in the foil, to rest and finish cooking in its own steam for about 15 minutes.

**4** Unwrap the salmon and carefully divide into portions, easing the fish from the bone as you do so. Serve at once.

This whole baked salmon is delicious served simply with new potatoes and mangetout or sugar snap peas.

# Roasted monkfish with saffron aïoli

Illustrated on previous pages

**Serves 4-6**

2 small monkfish tails, each
   600g/1lb 5oz, filleted and skinned
   (ie. 4 fillets in total)
salt and pepper
4 fresh rosemary twigs
4-6 lemon slices
2 tbsp olive oil

**For the marinade**

4 garlic cloves, crushed
1½ tsp finely chopped fresh
   rosemary
1½ tsp ground coriander

1½ tsp ground cumin
2 tsp sweet paprika
4 tbsp finely chopped fresh
   coriander leaves
2 tbsp white wine
4 tbsp olive oil

**For the saffron aïoli**

2 garlic cloves
¼ tsp saffron strands
1 egg yolk
200ml/7fl oz olive oil
2 tbsp lemon juice (approximately)

**1** To make the marinade, pound the garlic, 1 tsp salt and the rosemary to a paste, using a pestle and mortar. Add the remaining ingredients and mix well. Cover and refrigerate.

**2** To make the aïoli, pound the garlic, saffron and ¼ tsp salt to a paste, then place in a blender with the egg yolk. With the motor running, slowly add the oil through the feeder tube until the aïoli is thick. Transfer to a bowl and stir in lemon juice to taste. Cover and chill.

**3** To prepare the monkfish, smear the flat side of two fillets with the marinade and sandwich together with the other fillets. Tie at intervals with cotton string and place in a shallow dish. Leave to marinate in a cool place for 2-3 hours.

**4** To cook, preheat oven to 220C/fan oven 200C/Gas 7. Place the fish on a rack in a roasting tin and season well. Thread the rosemary twigs and lemon slices through the string. Drizzle with the 2 tbsp oil and roast for 20 minutes or until cooked through.

**5** Leave the monkfish to rest for 5-10 minutes before serving, with the saffron aïoli and potato chips.

# Skate with nutty brown butter

½ red onion, finely chopped
6 tbsp cider vinegar
4 cleaned skate wings, each about
   200g/7oz
3 pints/1.7 litres court bouillon
   (see note)

1 tsp yellow mustard seeds
50g/2oz unsalted butter
4 tbsp finely chopped fresh parsley
caper berries or capers, to garnish

**1** Put the chopped red onion into a small bowl, pour on the cider vinegar
and set aside to marinate.
**2** Place the skate wings in a large shallow pan and add sufficient court
bouillon to just cover them. Slowly bring to the boil, then immediately lower
the heat until the liquid is barely moving. Poach the skate wings for about
10 minutes until the flesh is no longer pink inside. Carefully lift out the
skate on to warmed plates; keep warm.
**3** Drain the onion and set aside, reserving the vinegar.
**4** Dry-fry the mustard seeds in a heavy-based frying pan over a high heat
until they begin to pop. Immediately add the butter and, as soon as it melts,
add the vinegar.
**5** Pour the sizzling butter over the skate wings and scatter with the red
onion and parsley. Garnish with caper berries or capers and serve at once.

**Note** To make a court bouillon, put 3 pints/1.7 litres water in a large
pan with ½ red onion, sliced, 6 peppercorns, 2 tsp salt, 6 mustard seeds
and 1 tbsp cider vinegar. Bring to the boil, lower the heat and simmer
for 5 minutes.

Skate wings have a delicate texture and a fine
flavour. For optimum results, soak the skate
in salted water in the fridge before poaching.
Take care to avoid overcooking.

# Smoked salmon and leek risotto

5 tbsp olive oil
450g/1lb medium leeks, thinly sliced
2 garlic cloves, finely chopped
500g/1lb 2oz arborio or other
  risotto rice
300ml/½ pint medium white wine
1 litre/2 pints well flavoured fish
  stock (approximately)

225g/8oz sliced smoked salmon,
  roughly chopped
salt and pepper
**To serve**
crème fraîche
lumpfish roe or salmon caviar
  (optional)

**1** Heat the olive oil in a heavy-based pan. Add the leeks and sauté for a few minutes until lightly coloured and beginning to soften. Stir in the garlic and cook for 2-3 minutes.
**2** Add the rice and stir well to coat with oil. Add the wine and boil until totally reduced.
**3** Meanwhile, bring the stock to a simmer in another pan.
**4** Add a large ladleful of stock to the rice and stir until it is absorbed. Continue to add the stock in this way, ensuring each addition is absorbed before adding more, until the rice is tender and creamy, but firm to the bite.
**5** Gently fold in the smoked salmon. Season generously with pepper and salt to taste. Cover and leave to rest for 1 minute. Serve topped with crème fraîche, and lumpfish roe or salmon caviar if wished.

A luxurious risotto flavoured with wine, sautéed leeks and lashings of smoked salmon. For a special supper, top with a spoonful of crème fraîche and a little lumpfish roe or salmon caviar.

# Mediterranean fish stew

Illustrated on previous pages

4 tbsp olive oil

1 onion, finely chopped

5 garlic cloves, finely chopped

1 small fennel bulb, finely chopped

3 celery sticks, finely chopped

400g can chopped tomatoes

1 tbsp fresh thyme leaves

1 bay leaf

grated rind and juice of ½ orange

5cm/2in strip of lemon peel

1 tsp saffron strands

700ml/1¼ pints fish stock (see note)

3 tbsp Pernod

250g/9oz thick cod fillet

250g/9oz sea bass or hoki fillet

250g/9oz raw tiger prawns, shelled
   and deveined

3 tbsp finely chopped fresh flat
   leaf parsley

salt and pepper

**1** Heat the oil in a large saucepan. Add the onion, garlic, fennel and celery and cook on a low heat, stirring occasionally, for 15-20 minutes until the vegetables are soft and just starting to colour.

**2** Add the tomatoes with their juice, thyme, bay leaf, orange rind and juice, lemon peel and saffron. Cook briskly for 5 minutes, then add the stock and Pernod and bring to the boil. Turn the heat down and simmer for 20 minutes.

**3** Meanwhile, cut the cod and sea bass into 5cm/2in cubes. Add to the pan and cook for 3 minutes, then add prawns and cook for a further 3 minutes.

**4** Stir in the chopped parsley and check the seasoning. Serve in warmed bowls with hot bread to mop up the delicious juices. Accompany with salad.

**Note** To make your own stock, ask your fishmonger for the fish bones and trimmings. Put in a pan with the prawn shells, 2-3 onion slices, a handful of parsley sprigs, a bay leaf and a few peppercorns. Add water to cover, bring to the boil and simmer for 20 minutes. Strain and use as required.

This version of the famous Mediterranean fish stew features cod, sea bass and tiger prawns.

# Chinese-style sea bass

1 bunch spring onions, finely
shredded
2 sea bass, each about 700g/1lb 9oz,
cleaned
1½ tsp Chinese five spice powder
3 garlic cloves, finely sliced

4cm/1½in piece fresh root ginger,
shredded
½ tsp black, or toasted white
sesame seeds
3 tbsp sunflower oil
5 tbsp light soy sauce

**1** Preheat oven to 230C/fan oven 210C/Gas 8. Put the shredded spring onion in a bowl, add some cold water to cover and chill in the fridge to curl the onion shreds.
**2** Make deep slashes in both sides of the fish, about 2.5cm/1in apart. Rub the spice powder into the cuts and inside the cavity. Place the sea bass on a large heatproof serving plate.
**3** Drain the spring onion; pat dry. Scatter the onion, garlic, ginger and sesame seeds over the fish. Place some scrunched up balls of foil over the base of a large roasting tin and carefully position the plate of fish on top. Pour over the oil and soy sauce.
**4** Pour a 4cm/1½in depth of boiling water into the roasting tin, then cover with foil to form a tent over the fish; secure the foil under the edge of the tin to hold in the steam during baking.
**5** Carefully place in the oven and bake for about 12-16 minutes, depending on size, until the sea bass is tender. Serve with rice and stir-fried vegetables.

**Note** The fish is cooked when the flesh divides into flakes easily.

An impressive steamed fish to bring to
the table whole. Serve with plain rice and
a colourful medley of stir-fried vegetables.

# Monkfish skewers

4 monkfish fillets, each 200g/7oz,
  skinned
juice of 1 small lemon
1 tsp fennel seeds
salt and pepper

4 shallots (unpeeled)
1 red pepper, cored, seeded and cut
  into 12 pieces
a little olive oil, for brushing
lemon wedges, to serve

**1** Cut each monkfish fillet into 5 or 6 pieces and place in a bowl with
the lemon juice, fennel seeds, salt and pepper; toss to mix and set aside.
**2** Put the shallots in a pan, cover with cold water and bring to the boil.
Simmer gently for 6-8 minutes, then drain and refresh in cold water.
Peel and quarter the shallots lengthways.
**3** Preheat the grill to medium. Thread the monkfish chunks onto 4 long
skewers, alternating with the red pepper and shallots.
**4** Brush with a little olive oil and grill for 12-15 minutes, turning the
skewers occasionally. Serve with lemon wedges, a leafy salad and warm bread.

Firm fleshed monkfish is the perfect choice
to thread onto skewers, as it doesn't easily
disintegrate. Ask the fishmonger to fillet and
skin the fish for you.

# Greek baked mackerel plaki

4 large mackerel, cleaned and trimmed
salt and pepper
juice of 2 lemons
3 garlic cloves, finely chopped
1 tsp fresh thyme leaves

4 plum tomatoes, skinned, seeded and diced
20 black olives, stoned and chopped
4 tbsp olive oil
5 tbsp dry white wine

**1** Cut 3 slashes on both sides of each fish and place in an oiled large, shallow ovenproof dish; season well. Pour over the lemon juice, cover and leave to marinate in a cool place for 1 hour, turning occasionally.
**2** Preheat oven to 190C/fan oven 170C/Mark 5. Spoon the remaining ingredients over the fish. Bake for 15-20 minutes, until cooked.
**3** Serve with rice and a green salad topped with crumbled feta and thin red onion slices.

Fresh mackerel baked with lemon, garlic, thyme, black olives and white wine – to delicious effect.

# Moroccan grilled cod

4 cod fillets, each 175-200g/6-7oz, skinned

**For the chermoula**

2 tbsp roughly chopped fresh coriander

1 tbsp chopped fresh mint

1 tbsp chopped fresh flat leaf parsley

2 garlic cloves, chopped

1 red chilli, seeded and chopped

1 tsp paprika

1½ tsp roasted cumin seeds

1 tsp saffron strands

5 tbsp olive oil

juice of 1 lemon

1½ tsp salt

**1** Place the fish fillets in a shallow ceramic or glass dish.

**2** Put the chermoula ingredients in a food processor and blend until smooth. Spoon over the fish and turn to coat. Cover and marinate in the fridge for at least 2 hours, ideally overnight, turning occasionally.

**3** Preheat grill to medium-high. Lift the fish out of the marinade and grill for 5-7 minutes on each side or until lightly browned and cooked through. Check the seasoning. Serve with warm pitta bread and yogurt.

Chermoula, a Moroccan spice and herb mix, transforms cod into an exciting dish.

# Seared tuna with fennel and thyme

4 tuna or swordfish steaks, each
  200g/7oz
salt and pepper
3 tbsp Pernod
2 tbsp olive oil
zest and juice of 1 lemon
2 tsp fresh thyme leaves
2 tsp fennel seeds, lightly roasted
4 sun-dried tomatoes, finely chopped
1 tsp dried chilli flakes

**For the tomato salsa**
4 plum tomatoes, skinned, seeded
  and sliced
2 tbsp shredded fresh basil leaves
1 red chilli, seeded and finely sliced
3 tbsp extra virgin olive oil
2 tsp balsamic vinegar
1 tsp caster sugar
**For the garnish**
thyme sprigs

**1** Season the fish and place in a shallow dish. In a bowl, mix together
the Pernod, olive oil, lemon zest and juice, thyme, fennel seeds, sun-dried
tomatoes and chilli. Pour over the fish, cover and leave to marinate
in a cool place for 1-2 hours.

**2** Meanwhile, combine the ingredients for the tomato salsa in a bowl. Season,
then cover and set aside to allow the flavours to infuse.

**3** To cook the fish, preheat a lightly oiled griddle or a heavy based frying
pan over a high heat. When very hot, cook the fish steaks for 3-4 minutes
on each side; they should still be a little pink in the middle.

**4** Transfer the fish steaks to warmed plates, garnish with thyme sprigs and
serve with the tomato salsa.

Hearty fresh tuna or swordfish steaks are
marinated with Mediterranean flavours, then
quickly seared on a hot griddle. A tomato and
basil salsa is the ideal complement.

# Seared salmon on lemon pasta salad

4 small skinless salmon fillets,
  each about 140g/5oz (see note)
225g/8oz dried fusilli or other
  pasta shapes
5 tbsp extra virgin olive oil
2 tsp fresh thyme leaves
1 tbsp lemon juice
1 tbsp black peppercorns, crushed
1 tsp cumin seeds

**For the salsa**
¼ tsp saffron strands
3 tomatoes, peeled, seeded and diced
3 spring onions, finely chopped
1 garlic clove, crushed
1 tbsp shredded fresh basil
salt and pepper
**For the garnish**
basil leaves

**1** First make the salsa. Soak the saffron in 1 tbsp boiling water for
10 minutes, then mix with the other salsa ingredients; set aside.
**2** Cook the pasta in boiling salted water until al dente.
**3** Meanwhile, in a small pan, warm 4 tbsp of the oil with the thyme, lemon
juice and seasoning. Drain the pasta thoroughly and toss with the dressing.
Leave to cool.
**4** Preheat a ridged griddle or heavy-based frying pan until very hot.
Combine the peppercorns and cumin seeds and press firmly onto the salmon
fillets. Brush with the remaining oil.
**5** Add the salmon to the griddle and sear for 1½ minutes each side. Remove
from the pan, let cool slightly, then slice thickly.
**6** Arrange the pasta salad on plates and top with the warm salmon slices.
Spoon around the saffron salsa and serve garnished with basil leaves.

**Note** Make sure that you use the freshest possible salmon for this dish.

Salmon is seared quickly over a high heat
so the outside is crisp and slightly charred,
whilst the centre remains rare and moist.

# Hoki, ham and gruyère grills

4 thick skinless hoki or cod fillets,
  each about 200g/7oz
salt and pepper
50g/2oz pitted green olives, sliced
100g/4oz gruyère cheese, finely
  grated
50g/2oz wafer-thin smoked ham

**1** Preheat the grill. Lay the fish fillets in a grillproof dish, season, then grill for 2-3 minutes. Mix the olives and cheese together.
**2** Turn the fish steaks over and top with the ham. Scatter with the cheese and olives.
**3** Grill for a further 4-5 minutes until the cheese is golden and bubbling and the fish fillets are cooked through to the middle. Serve with a salad and crusty bread.

Hoki, a relative of hake, is fished from the seas around New Zealand and makes an excellent alternative to cod.

# Saltimbocca of sole

2 lemon sole, filleted and skinned
8 slices of Parma ham
16 basil leaves
pepper
50g/2oz unsalted butter
150ml/¼ pint chicken stock

150ml/¼ pint double cream
4 tbsp white wine
1 tsp Dijon mustard
1 tbsp finely chopped fresh flat leaf
   parsley

**1** Preheat oven to 200C/fan oven 180C/Gas 6. Trim the sole fillets, then cut each in half lengthways.
**2** Lay the slices of Parma ham on a board, place 2 basil leaves on each and cover with a sole fillet. Season with pepper. Starting from the tail end, roll up fairly tightly, making sure the fish is covered by the ham. Repeat to make the remaining rolls.
**3** Melt 25g/1oz of the butter in a large frying pan. When sizzling, carefully add the fish rolls, seam side down, and cook for 1-2 minutes on each side, until golden brown.
**4** Carefully place the rolls, seam side down, on a baking tray lined with greaseproof paper and bake for 8-10 minutes.
**5** Meanwhile, make the sauce. Put the stock, cream, wine and mustard in a small pan and bring to the boil, stirring. Simmer for 4-5 minutes until reduced and slightly thickened, then whisk in the remaining butter. Season with pepper to taste and add the parsley.
**6** To serve, spoon the sauce onto 4 warmed plates and arrange 2 saltimboccas on each plate. Serve at once, with fluffy mashed potatoes and wilted spring greens.

Lemon sole fillets are wrapped in Parma ham and served with a delicious mild creamy mustard sauce.

# Salmon with ginger and coriander

Illustrated on previous pages

**Serves 3-4; or 8 as a starter**
500g/1lb 2oz salmon fillet (tail end),
  with skin
25g/1oz fresh root ginger, peeled
40g/1½oz fresh coriander leaves,
  chopped

1 tsp coriander seeds
1 tbsp sea salt
1 tbsp caster sugar
freshly ground black pepper

**1** Trim the salmon, removing any small bones with tweezers.
**2** Coarsely chop the ginger and squeeze out the juice on to the salmon, using a garlic press. Mix the remaining ingredients together and press on to both sides of the fish.
**3** Lay the fish, skin side down, in a shallow dish large enough to hold it flat. Cover with baking parchment, place a board on top and weight down. Leave to marinate in the fridge for 3-4 days, turning the fish each day.
**4** Blot excess oil from the fish with kitchen paper. Slice thinly, on the diagonal, off the skin. Serve with rocket and rye bread.

Very fresh salmon is essential for this raw marinated dish.

# Italian seafood risotto

3 tbsp extra virgin olive oil
3 garlic cloves, finely chopped
200g/7oz salmon fillet, skinned
  and cut into 2.5cm/1in cubes
250g/9oz raw tiger prawns, shelled
  and deveined
4 baby squid, cleaned and cut
  into rings
125ml/4fl oz dry white wine
1.5 litres/2¾ pints fish stock

40g/1½oz butter
4 shallots, finely chopped
½ red pepper, cored, seeded and diced
1 plum tomato, skinned, seeded and
  chopped
400g/14oz arborio rice
salt and pepper
2 tbsp finely chopped fresh flat
  leaf parsley

**1** Heat 2 tbsp of the oil in a large saucepan, add the garlic and sauté for
1 minute. Add the salmon, prawns and squid and stir-fry for 3 minutes,
then add the wine and bring to a simmer. Remove the fish and shellfish
with a slotted spoon and set aside.

**2** Add the fish stock to the pan; set aside.

**3** Melt 25g/1oz of the butter in another large pan with the remaining oil.
Add the shallots and cook until golden. Add the red pepper, tomato and rice;
cook, stirring, for 2 minutes.

**4** Meanwhile, bring the stock to a simmer. Gradually stir the stock into the
rice mixture, about 125ml/4fl oz at a time, ensuring each addition is
absorbed before adding more. Continue until the rice is tender. With the last
addition of stock, add the seafood and season to taste.

**5** Stir in the remaining butter and chopped parsley. Serve at once.

**Note** The cooking time is about 20 minutes, from the first addition of the
stock. Depending on the variety of rice, you may need to use a little less
or more liquid.

A creamy, wine enriched risotto, liberally
flavoured with fresh salmon, tiger prawns
and baby squid.

# smart
# chicken

# Chargrilled chicken stacks with basil

**Serves 4**

4 free-range chicken breast
  fillets, skinned
1 large red pepper
1 large yellow pepper
2 medium-small aubergines
salt and pepper
5 tbsp extra virgin olive oil

**For the basil dressing**

16 fresh basil leaves, roughly torn
2 tbsp cider vinegar
6 tbsp olive oil
½ tsp Dijon mustard

**For the garnish**

basil leaves

**1** Using a sharp knife, slice each chicken breast into 3 even medallions.
**2** Cut off the tops and a little of the base from the peppers, then cut each
one into four, to give even, flat pieces; discard seeds. Cut the aubergine
into 12 even slices, about 5mm/¼ inch thick.
**3** Put the chicken and vegetables in a large shallow dish, season and pour
over the oil. Mix well, cover and leave to marinate in a cool place for at least
30 minutes (or up to 3 hours).
**4** Put the dressing ingredients in a blender, season and pulse until
amalgamated but retaining some flecks of basil.
**5** Preheat a chargrill pan, or grill, to high. Sear the chicken and vegetables
in batches to obtain a charred effect on both sides; turn down the heat to
cook right through.
**6** To assemble, halve the pepper pieces. Place a chicken medallion on each
plate and stack the vegetables and remaining chicken medallions on top,
alternating the colours and finishing with yellow pepper. Serve hot or cold,
drizzled with the dressing and garnished with basil leaves.

**Note** The stacks can be assembled ahead in a deep dish, covered and warmed
through in the oven to serve.

Serve these chicken stacks with flavoured
breads and a leafy salad.

# Aubergine and chicken 'roulades'

Illustrated on previous pages

450g/1lb skinless chicken breast
   fillets, or skinned boneless thighs,
   or a mixture
1 rounded tbsp half fat crème fraîche
2 tbsp finely shredded fresh basil
salt and pepper
2 medium-large aubergines
oil, for brushing

**For the tomato sauce**
2 tsp olive oil
1 small onion or 2 shallots,
   finely chopped
1 garlic clove, crushed
500ml/18fl oz passata
few basil leaves
1 tbsp red or white wine

**1** Mince the chicken meat or finely chop in a food processor; transfer
to a bowl. Mix in the crème fraîche, basil, salt and pepper.

**2** Thinly slice the aubergines lengthwise, to give 10-12 slices from each;
discard the outer skin-covered slices. Brush one side of each aubergine slice
with a little oil and place, oiled-side down, on a work surface.

**3** Divide the chicken mixture between the aubergine slices and spread evenly,
almost to the edges. Roll up the aubergine slices to enclose the filling and
thread onto 4 wooden kebab skewers. Place on a non-stick baking sheet.
Preheat oven to 190C/fan oven 170C/ Gas 5.

**4** To make the sauce, heat the oil in a pan and fry the onion for 3-4 minutes
until softened, then add the garlic and cook for 1 minute. Add the passata,
basil leaves and wine. Bring to the boil, reduce the heat and simmer gently
for about 10 minutes. Season to taste.

**5** Meanwhile, cook the aubergine rolls in the oven for about 20-25 minutes,
until the chicken is cooked through, turning halfway through the cooking
time. Serve with the tomato sauce and a leafy green salad.

Oven-baked aubergine slices rolled around
a tasty minced chicken filling.

# Pan-fried chicken with shiitake

25g/1oz unsalted butter
4 chicken breast fillets (with skin)
2 garlic cloves, finely chopped
150g/5½ oz small shiitake
  mushrooms
4 tbsp extra dry white vermouth

300ml/½ pint carton fresh
  chicken stock
4 tbsp crème fraîche
salt and pepper
4 spring onions, shredded

**1** Melt the butter in a large frying pan. Add the chicken and cook gently for 5 minutes, turning once. Remove and set aside.
**2** Add the garlic and mushrooms to the pan; stir-fry until the mushrooms start to soften.
**3** Add the vermouth and stock. Increase the heat and boil rapidly until the liquid has almost totally evaporated.
**4** Stir in the crème fraîche, season, then return the chicken to the pan. Part cover and simmer for 5 minutes or until the chicken is cooked through. Stir in the spring onions and heat through. Serve with tagliatelle.

Pan-fried chicken readily takes on flavours and cooks quickly, so it's perfect for a fast midweek supper.

# Golden tapenade supremes

Illustrated on previous pages

4 chicken supremes (see note)
85g/3oz ricotta cheese
4 tbsp black olive tapenade
4 sun-dried tomatoes in oil, chopped
salt and pepper
olive oil, for brushing

**1** Preheat oven to 200C/fan oven 180C/Gas 6. Break up the ricotta in a bowl, then beat in the tapenade, sun-dried tomatoes and salt and pepper to taste.
**2** Loosen the skin covering each chicken breast and push in as much stuffing as will fit between the skin and the flesh. Gently reform the skin over the stuffing and chicken.
**3** Brush the skin with olive oil and season well. Place in a baking dish and bake in the oven for 25 minutes.
**4** Allow the chicken to rest for 5 minutes before serving, with roasted peppers and new potatoes or rice.

**Note** Chicken supremes are breast fillets with the wing bone still attached – available ready-prepared from larger supermarkets. Alternatively ask your butcher to prepare them for you.

**Variation** Add a spoonful of chopped capers to the stuffing to cut the richness and add a delicious piquancy.

Cut into these moist chicken breasts to reveal a soft, savoury stuffing – reminiscent of the flavours of Provence.

# Coq au vin with thyme and juniper

2-3 tbsp olive oil
8 smoked streaky bacon rashers,
   halved and rolled up
250g/9oz shallots, peeled (see note)
250g/9oz baby button mushrooms
8 boneless chicken thighs, skinned
2 tbsp seasoned flour
300ml/½ pint Beaujolais

2 tbsp brandy
300ml/½ pint chicken stock
1 tbsp tomato purée
2 garlic cloves, chopped
4 juniper berries, crushed
1 tbsp fresh thyme leaves
salt and pepper

**1** Preheat oven to 180C/fan oven 160C/Gas 4. Heat 2 tbsp olive oil in a large heavy-based frying pan and fry the bacon rolls for a few minutes until turning golden; transfer to a flameproof casserole, using a slotted spoon.
**2** Fry the shallots and mushrooms in the oil left in the pan for a few minutes, turning, until slightly coloured. Add to the casserole.
**3** Coat the chicken thighs in the seasoned flour, then fry for about 5 minutes until golden, adding more oil to the pan if necessary. Transfer to the casserole.
**4** Pour the wine, brandy and stock into the pan. Stir in the tomato purée, garlic, juniper and thyme. Bring to the boil, then pour over the chicken.
**5** Cover tightly and cook the casserole in the oven for 1 hour or until the chicken and shallots are tender; check the seasoning. If preparing ahead, cool and keep in the fridge for up to 2 days.
**6** When ready to serve, reheat on the hob until bubbling. Serve with green beans and sautéed potatoes.

**Note** Before peeling shallots, immerse in boiling water for 5 minutes – you will find the skins come away much more easily.

Juniper berries add an intriguing and subtle fragrance to this version of a classic, which is ideal for entertaining.

# Pan-seared chicken with garlic sauce

50g/2oz butter
4 boneless chicken breasts
  (with skin)
12 garlic cloves, unpeeled
300ml/½ pint dry or medium
  white wine

2 large fresh rosemary sprigs
2 fresh bay leaves
salt and pepper

**1** Melt the butter in a sauté pan. When foaming, add the chicken skin-side down and the unpeeled garlic cloves. Fry for about 5 minutes, then turn the chicken over.

**2** Add the wine and herbs. Season, then cover tightly and simmer for 20 minutes. Transfer the chicken to a warmed plate and leave to rest in a warm place.

**3** Mash most of the garlic into the sauce using a potato masher, then bring to the boil, taste and season. Strain the sauce over the chicken, or pour it over – bits and all! Serve with sugar snaps or mangetout and new potatoes.

A real must for garlic lovers – whole cloves are cooked with chicken fillets, then mashed into the sauce to flavour and thicken it.

# Tandoori chicken pieces

Illustrated on previous pages

8-12 skinless chicken pieces (thighs, drumsticks, halved breasts)
juice of 1 lemon
sea salt
**For the marinade**
250ml/9fl oz yogurt
1 onion, cut into chunks
3 garlic cloves, crushed

2.5cm/1in piece fresh root ginger, chopped
2 tbsp turmeric
1 green chilli, seeded
1 tbsp garam masala
**To serve**
lime wedges

**1** Cut deep slits in the meatiest parts of the chicken pieces and place in a shallow dish. Sprinkle with lemon juice and salt and let stand for 30 minutes.

**2** Meanwhile, whizz all the marinade ingredients together in a food processor or blender to form a smooth paste. Add the chicken pieces and toss to coat. Cover and leave to marinate in a cool place for several hours, or overnight if possible.

**3** Preheat a baking sheet in the oven at 250C/fan oven 230C/Gas 9. Lift the chicken out of the marinade and place the drumsticks and thighs on the hot baking sheet. Bake for about 20 minutes, adding the chicken breast pieces after about 5 minutes.

**4** Serve with lime wedges and warm naan bread or rice.

**Note** An Indian-style salad of tomato, cucumber and chopped onion, scattered with plenty of chopped fresh coriander is the ideal accompaniment.

For optimum flavour, slash the chicken pieces and then leave to marinate in the tandoori mixture overnight.

# Basil-wrapped chicken with porcini stuffing

4 chicken breast fillets, with skin

**For the stuffing**

15g/½oz dried porcini (or other
  dried mushrooms)

1 tbsp olive oil

1 small garlic clove, crushed

1 shallot, finely diced

75g/3oz chestnut mushrooms,
  finely chopped

50g/2oz creamy soft goat's cheese

2 tbsp chopped fresh parsley

salt and pepper

25g/1oz unsalted butter, softened

12 large basil leaves

squeeze of lemon juice

100ml/3½fl oz dry white wine

**1** Preheat the oven to 200C/ fan oven 180C/Gas 6. Put the dried mushrooms into a small bowl, pour on just enough warm water to cover and set aside to soak for 15 minutes.

**2** Meanwhile, loosen the skin from one side of each chicken breast, working your fingers under the skin, keeping it attached on the opposite side.

**3** Drain the porcini, reserving the soaking liquor, and chop finely. Heat the olive oil in a heavy-based frying pan, add the garlic and shallot and cook gently for 5 minutes or until softened. Add the fresh and dried mushrooms and cook until softened and almost dry. Take off the heat and cool slightly.

**4** Add the goat's cheese and parsley to the stuffing, and season well with salt and pepper. Mix until evenly combined, then leave to cool completely.

**5** When the stuffing is cold, carefully spoon it under the chicken breast skin with a teaspoon and spread evenly. Push a fine wooden skewer through the skin and breast along the open side to secure. Put the chicken breasts, skin-side uppermost and side by side, in a small roasting tin.

**6** Smear the butter over the skin and lay the basil leaves on top. Season with salt and pepper and sprinkle with lemon juice. Pour the reserved mushroom liquor into the tin, leaving behind the sediment, then add the wine. Bake for 25 minutes or until the chicken is cooked through, basting occasionally.

**7** Serve the chicken breasts drizzled with the pan juices and accompanied by courgettes and new potatoes or rice.

**Note** Choose chicken breast fillets that are generously covered with skin, which is intact, to hold the stuffing in place.

# Chicken with caramelised apples

**Serves 6**

6 corn-fed chicken breast fillets
  (with skin)
salt and pepper
50g/2oz unsalted butter
150ml/¼ pint double cream

3 large Cox's apples, about 500g/1lb
  in total
2 tbsp sunflower oil
400g/14oz shallots, peeled
3 tbsp Calvados or brandy

**1** Preheat oven to 190C/fan oven 170C/Gas 5. Season the chicken with salt and pepper.

**2** Melt half the butter in a flameproof casserole. Add the chicken skin side down and fry for about 3 minutes until golden brown. Turn and brown the other side.

**3** Add half the cream, cover and cook in the oven for 20-25 minutes.

**4** Meanwhile quarter, core and slice the apples. Heat the oil in a large heavy-based frying pan and fry the shallots for 8 minutes until browned. Add remaining butter and fry the apples for about 5 minutes, turning, until evenly golden; keep warm.

**5** Remove casserole from oven and place on a high heat. Pour in the remaining cream and let bubble for 1 minute. Add half the apples and shallots. Add the Calvados, cover and turn off the heat.

**6** Pile the remaining shallots and apples on top of the chicken and drizzle with the sauce to serve.

A delicious brew of rich flavours just begging to be piled onto a mound of mashed celeriac and potatoes.

# Bronzed paprika chicken

Illustrated on previous pages

**Serves 4-6**

1 oven-ready chicken, about
   1.6kg/3½lb
salt and pepper
1 unwaxed lemon, halved
small sprig of fresh bay leaves
50g/2oz butter, softened
4 tsp paprika

¼ tsp cayenne pepper
2-3 whole garlic bulbs, halved
   crosswise
1 tbsp olive oil
450g/1lb cherry tomatoes on the vine
70g/2½oz finely sliced chorizo
   sausage
bay leaves, to garnish

**1** Remove any excess fat from the cavity of the chicken and season. Place the lemon halves and bay leaves inside.

**2** Loosen the skin away from the chicken breast and legs, then smear the butter onto the flesh under the skin to keep it moist. Mix the paprika, ¼ tsp salt, ¼ tsp pepper and the cayenne together. Rub this mixture all over the skin. Tie the legs together and put the chicken on a trivet in a large roasting tin.

**3** Preheat oven to 190C/fan oven 170C/Gas 5. Estimate the cooking time, allowing 20 minutes per 450g/lb, plus 20 minutes. Toss the garlic in a little olive oil and place around the bird. Roast in the oven, basting occasionally.

**4** About 10 minutes before the end of the roasting time, toss the cherry tomatoes in the remaining olive oil and add to the roasting tin.

**5** Ensure chicken is cooked by piercing the thickest part of the leg with a skewer: the juices should be clear and golden; if pink, roast for a little longer.

**6** Transfer to a warmed platter and rest for 10-15 minutes. Meanwhile, fry the chorizo slices in a dry pan over a high heat until crisp. Scatter on top of the chicken and surround with tomatoes and garlic. Garnish with bay leaves.

You can prepare the chicken for roasting a few hours ahead. Keep in the fridge, but bring to room temperature before cooking.

# Maple roast poussins with thyme

4 poussins (baby chicken)
6 tbsp maple syrup
1 tbsp Dijon mustard
3 garlic cloves, crushed
1½ tsp fresh lemon thyme leaves
salt and pepper

**1** Preheat oven to 220C/fan oven 200C/Gas 7. Halve the poussins lengthways along the breast bone, using poultry shears or kitchen scissors, and remove the tips from the wings and knuckles. Place in a large dish.
**2** Mix together the maple syrup, mustard, garlic, lemon thyme and seasoning until well blended. Spoon over the poussins and turn them in the mixture to coat all over.
**3** Arrange the poussins, close together, in a large roasting dish and spoon over the remaining juices. Roast for 25-30 minutes until golden. Serve with creamy mashed potato and green vegetables.

Less sweet than honey, maple syrup marries with the citrus fragrance of lemon thyme to add succulence and flavour to poussins.

# Spicy chicken cakes

Illustrated on previous pages

**Serves 3-4**

350g/12oz minced chicken
2 tbsp Thai red curry paste
1 medium egg, beaten
2 tbsp cornflour
2 tbsp chopped fresh coriander

2 kaffir lime leaves (see note),
  finely shredded
2 spring onions, finely sliced
1 red chilli, seeded and finely sliced
oil for deep-frying

**1** Put the minced chicken, red curry paste and about half of the egg in
a food processor; work until evenly blended. Transfer to a mixing bowl.
**2** Add the cornflour, coriander, lime leaves, spring onions and chilli. Mix
well, using your fingers, adding more egg as necessary to bind the mixture.
**3** Divide the mixture into 12 portions and roll each into a ball. Mould and
flatten each ball into a 'cake' about 5cm/2in in diameter and 5-7mm/¼in thick.
**4** Heat a 5cm/2in depth of oil in a wok or deep frying pan. Deep-fry the
cakes, a few at a time, for about 5 minutes, until lightly browned and cooked.
**5** Drain on crumpled kitchen paper and serve hot with a salsa, as an
appetiser or with a salad as a starter or light lunch.

**Note** Kaffir lime leaves are available in packs of mixed Thai flavourings from
some supermarkets. If unobtainable, use the grated zest of 2 limes.

These tasty morsels are great as an appetiser
with drinks. Serve with a fresh tomato,
cucumber, coriander and red onion salsa –
spiked with lime juice.

# Tuscan chicken thighs

4-6 garlic cloves, peeled
2 tsp sea salt
1 tsp freshly ground black pepper
3 tbsp finely chopped fresh rosemary
12 boneless chicken thighs, skinned

12 thin slices pancetta or
 streaky bacon
12 fresh bay leaves
olive oil, for brushing

**1** Pound the garlic with the salt, pepper and rosemary, using a pestle and mortar or coffee grinder. Rub this paste generously all over the flesh-side of the chicken thighs.
**2** Re-shape and wrap each thigh in a slice of pancetta, tucking in a bay leaf. Secure with fine string. Preheat the grill.
**3** Place the chicken in the grill pan and brush with olive oil. Grill for 15-20 minutes, turning every 5 minutes until golden, crisp and cooked through. Serve drizzled with extra olive oil and accompanied by a salad.

Rosemary, garlic and plenty of seasoning give these succulent chicken thighs an authentic Tuscan flavour.

# Spicy chicken korma with cashews

2 onions, quartered
4 garlic cloves
7.5cm/3in piece fresh root ginger, chopped
100g/4oz cashew nuts
3 tbsp sunflower oil
2 red chillies, seeded and sliced
1 tsp cumin seeds
1 tsp ground turmeric

1 tsp ground white pepper
700ml/1¼ pints chicken stock
4 skinless chicken breast fillets, cubed
150g/5oz carton yogurt
2 bananas, sliced
3 tbsp chopped fresh coriander
coriander sprigs, to garnish

**1** Put the onions, garlic, ginger and nuts in a food processor and blend to a paste.
**2** Heat the oil in a large frying pan, add the onion and cashew mixture with the chilli and cumin and fry for 10 minutes, stirring frequently.
**3** Stir in the turmeric and pepper, then pour in the stock and simmer for 5 minutes.
**4** Add the chicken, cover and simmer gently for 15 minutes.
**5** Stir in the yogurt, bananas and coriander. Garnish with sprigs of coriander and serve with basmati rice or naan bread.

Fresh ginger and chillies impart flavour, while ground cashew nuts give this curry an intriguing texture.

# Pancetta-wrapped roast chicken

1 oven-ready chicken, about
  1.5kg/3¼lb
200g/7oz Italian-style sausages,
  skinned
200g/7oz cooked chestnuts (ideally
  roasted), roughly chopped

salt and pepper
10 thin slices pancetta
oil, for brushing

**1** Preheat oven to 200C/fan oven 180C/Gas 6. Break up the sausage meat
with a fork and mix with the chestnuts and plenty of pepper. Use to stuff the
neck end of the chicken (not the cavity). Secure the flap under the bird with
a cocktail stick.
**2** Season the chicken with plenty of pepper, then lay the pancetta slices,
overlapping slightly, over the surface of the chicken.
**3** Put the chicken on a trivet in a roasting dish. Cover with a piece of oiled
baking parchment, securing at each 'corner' of the chicken with a cocktail
stick. Roast for 50 minutes, then carefully remove the paper. Roast for
a further 30-40 minutes until the chicken is cooked.

**Notes** To calculate roasting time, weigh the chicken and allow 20 minutes
per 500g/1lb, plus an extra 20 minutes at 190-200C/fan oven 180C/Gas 5-6.
To test that a roast chicken is cooked, pierce the thickest part of the leg with
a skewer and make sure that the juices run clear.

Tasty chicken with an Italian stuffing, roasted
in a crisp pancetta overcoat.

# Thai grilled chicken with coriander

Illustrated on previous pages

4 corn-fed chicken breasts
(with skin)
2 garlic cloves, chopped
100g/4oz fresh coriander leaves,
chopped
25g/1oz fresh mint leaves, chopped
2 tsp ground cumin
2 tsp ground coriander

1 red chilli, sliced
juice and grated rind of 1 lime
2 tsp soft brown sugar
250ml/9fl oz coconut milk
2 tsp sea salt
rocket leaves, to garnish
lime wedges, to serve

**1** Lay the chicken breasts, skin side up, on a board. With a sharp knife, make 3-4 shallow cuts in each one. Place the chicken breasts in a shallow dish, in which they fit snugly.
**2** Put all the remaining ingredients into a food processor, and blend until fairly smooth. Pour this marinade over the chicken and turn each piece to coat thoroughly. Cover and leave to marinate for at least 1 hour.
**3** Preheat the grill to high. Remove the chicken from the marinade and place, skin side up, on a lightly oiled grill pan. Grill for 8-10 minutes or until browned, then turn, baste with the marinade and grill the other side for 6-8 minutes or until cooked through.
**4** Serve hot, garnished with rocket leaves and accompanied by lime wedges, steamed Thai fragrant rice flavoured with coriander, and a green salad.

Grilled to a crust, these fragrant chicken portions are deliciously moist within.

# Thai-style risotto

2 tbsp sunflower oil
6 spring onions, finely sliced
1 lemon grass stalk, finely sliced
1 tsp crushed garlic
1 tsp finely grated fresh root ginger
350g/12oz arborio (risotto) rice
300g/10oz chicken breast, cut into
    2 cm/¾in cubes

100g/4oz shiitake mushrooms, sliced
1.2 litres/2 pints good quality
    chicken stock (see note)
4 tbsp chopped fresh coriander
salt and pepper
shredded spring onion, to garnish

**1** Heat the oil in a large heavy-based saucepan. Add the spring onions, lemon grass, garlic and ginger and stir-fry for 1 minute.
**2** Add the rice and cook, stirring, for a few minutes, then add the chicken and mushrooms. Stir-fry for a further 2-3 minutes.
**3** Add a ladleful of the stock and cook gently, stirring frequently, until it is absorbed. Continue adding the stock, a ladleful at a time as each addition is absorbed, until the rice is creamy in texture.
**4** Add the remaining stock and coriander. Season well, and stir over a low heat for a few minutes longer or until the rice is just tender and moist.
**5** Serve immediately, garnished with shredded spring onion.

**Note** Use homemade stock or buy a carton of fresh chicken stock.

Subtle eastern flavours give this Italian classic an original Thai twist.

# Saffron roast chicken

1 oven-ready chicken, about
  1.6kg/3½lb

**For the saffron butter**

50g/2oz unsalted butter, softened

½ packet saffron threads, crumbled

½ tsp salt

**For the onions**

1 tbsp olive oil

25g/1oz butter

450g/1lb onions, halved and
  thinly sliced

2 tsp garam masala

2 tsp cumin seeds

6 cardamom pods, lightly crushed

2 tsp finely chopped fresh root
  ginger

50g/2oz sultanas

**1** Preheat oven to 200C/fan oven 180C/Gas 6. Loosen the skin from the chicken breast by easing your fingers under the neck flap, over the breast and down to the legs, without puncturing the skin.

**2** Mix the ingredients for the saffron butter and spread evenly over the chicken breast under the skin. Secure the neck flap under the bird with a cocktail stick.

**3** Heat the oil and butter in a wide pan and gently fry the onions until softened. Add all the spices and cook for 2-3 minutes. Add the sultanas, then transfer to a roasting dish and place the chicken on top, breast side down. Roast for 45 minutes.

**4** Lower setting to 190C/fan oven 170C/Gas 5 and turn the chicken breast side up. Stir the onions, piling some of the lighter ones on top of the chicken to keep it moist. Roast for a further 45 minutes or until the chicken is cooked through and the onions are crisp and brown.

**Note** Roasting the chicken breast-side down to start with helps to keep the breast meat succulent and moist.

Saffron butter basted chicken roasted on a bed of sliced onion flavoured with spices.

# Steamed Thai chicken parcels

Illustrated on previous pages

4 large banana leaves (see note)
1 tbsp vegetable oil
4 spring onions, thinly sliced
1 tsp finely grated fresh root ginger
2 lemon grass stalks, thinly sliced

2 skinless chicken breast fillets, cut
   into 2cm/¾in cubes
100g/4oz shiitake mushrooms, sliced
2 tbsp soy sauce
175g/6oz basmati rice, cooked

**1** Trim the banana leaves to 20cm/8inch squares and set aside.
**2** Heat the oil in a large frying pan and sauté the spring onions, ginger
and lemon grass for 2-3 minutes. Add the chicken and mushrooms, and
stir-fry for 2 minutes. Add the soy sauce and cooked rice, and cook, stirring,
for 1 minute.
**3** Divide the mixture between the banana leaves and fold over to enclose the
filling; secure the parcels with bamboo skewers or twine. Place in a bamboo
steamer over a wok, or in a metal steamer, and steam for 15 minutes.
**4** Serve on warmed plates, allowing guests to open up their own parcels.

**Note** If banana leaves are unobtainable, lightly oiled baking parchment
squares can be used instead, but the flavour won't be quite the same.

Banana leaves, lemon grass, spring onions,
ginger and shiitake mushrooms give these
aromatic parcels their distinctive character.

# Chicken saltimbocca

4 slices prosciutto
12 large fresh sage leaves
4 skinless chicken breast fillets
salt and pepper
1 tbsp olive oil

large knob of butter
1 red onion, sliced
dash of white wine
4 tbsp crème fraîche

**1** Lay the prosciutto slices on a surface and place a sage leaf on each.
Position the chicken breasts at an angle on top and season with pepper. Top
with another sage leaf and wrap the chicken breasts in the prosciutto slices.
**2** Heat the oil and butter in a heavy-based frying pan, add the parcels and
fry for 2-3 minutes until lightly browned. Turn the parcels over and add the
rest of the sage. Fry for 2 minutes until the sage leaves are frazzled; remove
these with a slotted spoon and set aside.
**3** Lower the heat, add the onion to the pan and cook gently until softened.
Turn the chicken parcels again. Add the wine, increasing the heat and
stirring to deglaze the pan.
**4** Lower the heat, stir in the crème fraîche and simmer gently for 2-3 minutes
or until the chicken is cooked through. Serve garnished with the frazzled
sage leaves.

These prosciutto and sage flavoured parcels
are typically served with tagliatelle.

# smart
# meat

# Seared beef, physalis fruit and onions

400g/14oz baby onions, peeled
3 tbsp olive oil
1kg/2¼lb piece beef fillet
salt and pepper
70g/2½oz physalis fruit
200ml/7fl oz Muscat de Beaume de
    Venise, or Sauternes

**1** Preheat oven to 230C/fan oven 210C/Gas 8. Put the onions in a roasting tin, add 1 tbsp of the oil and toss to coat. Roast for 10 minutes.
**2** Meanwhile, pat the beef fillet dry with kitchen paper, rub with 1 tbsp of oil and season well.
**3** Preheat a heavy based frying pan, add the beef and brown on all sides over a high heat for about 5 minutes. Transfer the beef to the roasting tin and roast with the onions for 15 minutes.
**4** Toss the physalis fruit in the remaining 1 tbsp oil. Add to the meat and roast for a further 7 minutes. Transfer the beef, onions and physalis to a warm serving dish and leave to rest in a warm place for about 15 minutes.
**5** Meanwhile, add the wine to the roasting tin, stirring to deglaze and bubble over a high heat for about 1 minute. Pour any meat juices that have collected in the serving dish into the roasting tin and heat through.
**6** Carve the beef into medium thick slices. Serve with physalis fruit and roast onions on a bed of celeriac and potato mash, drizzled with the meat juices.

Serve this tender beef, crowned with the physalis fruit in their papery husks, on a mound of potato and celeriac mash with the sweet roast onions and rich meat juices.

# Mustard steaks on mushrooms

**Serves 2**
2 fillet steaks, each 175g/6oz
salt and pepper
2 tsp wholegrain mustard
2 tsp black olive paste
2 large flat mushrooms, about
   10cm/4in across

**For the vegetable julienne**
½ each red and yellow pepper,
   seeded and cut into fine strips
50g/2oz celeriac, cut into very
   fine strips

**1** Preheat oven to 240C/fan oven 220C/Gas 9. Using a sharp knife, score the steaks in a criss cross pattern at 1cm/½in intervals, cutting just less than halfway through depth.

**2** Mix together the mustard and olive paste and spread over the meat and into the cuts. Place the steaks, mustard side down, on a foil lined baking tray. Cook under a preheated high grill for about 3 minutes.

**3** Put the mushrooms, flat side up, on the baking tray. Turn the steaks over and carefully place on top of the mushrooms. Bake in the oven for 10 minutes or until the mushrooms are cooked through; the steaks should still be pink in the middle. (For well done steaks cook for 2 to 3 minutes longer.)

**4** Quickly toss together the vegetable julienne and pile on top of the steaks. Serve at once, with a salad.

A highly seasoned juicy steak cooked without extra fat and served with a crunchy julienne of vegetables.

# Whisky braised beef with pecans

Illustrated on previous pages

4 lean, thick braising steaks, about
   800g/1¾ lb in total
3-4 tbsp seasoned flour
1 tbsp olive oil
25g/1oz butter
2 garlic cloves, thinly sliced
250g/9oz shallots, peeled

2 fresh bay leaves, crushed
200g/7oz smoked bacon lardons
4 tbsp whisky
425ml/¾ pint beef stock
50g/2oz pecan nuts
3 tbsp chopped fresh parsley

**1** Preheat oven to 180C/fan oven 160C/Gas 4. Coat the steaks with the seasoned flour.
**2** Heat the oil and half the butter in a large frying pan and fry the steaks until sealed on both sides. Transfer to a shallow casserole.
**3** Add the garlic, shallots, bay leaves and half of the lardons to the frying pan; stir-fry until browned. Add the whisky, bubble to reduce, then stir in the stock, scraping up any sediment from the base of the pan. Pour over the beef.
**4** Cover and braise in the oven for two hours until tender. If preparing ahead, cool, then cover and chill for up to 3 days, or freeze.
**5** To serve, defrost at cool room temperature overnight (if frozen). Reheat in a pan until piping hot. Fry the rest of the lardons in the remaining butter until golden. Add the pecans and cook for a few minutes. Stir in the parsley.
**6** Serve the beef casserole topped with the pecan mix. Accompany with creamy mashed potato and a green vegetable, such as braised cabbage.

Braising steaks are cooked with a tot of whisky, whole shallots and smoky bacon, then served topped with a buttery mix of toasted pecans and crisp fried bacon.

# Charred pepper and steak tacos

4 tbsp olive oil

4 tsp Cajun spice seasoning

2 sirloin steaks, each 175g/6oz, cut into strips

2 garlic cloves, crushed

4 yellow peppers, seeded and thinly sliced

3 red onions, sliced

12 small taco shells

two 220g cans refried beans

4 tbsp fresh coriander leaves, chopped

300ml/½ pint soured cream

**1** Mix half the oil with the spice in a shallow dish. Add the steak and toss well; set aside.

**2** Heat remaining oil in a wok and stir-fry the garlic, peppers and onions over a high heat for 8-10 minutes until lightly charred. Add the steak and stir-fry for 4-5 minutes.

**3** Meanwhile warm the tacos and beans according to the packet instructions. Stir the chopped coriander into the soured cream.

**4** Spoon the beans into the taco shells. Top with the pepper mixture and flavoured soured cream.

Mexican taco shells are filled with steak strips, charred peppers and refried beans, then topped with soured cream flavoured with coriander.

# Fillet of beef teriyaki

450g/1lb piece beef fillet (from the
  tail end)
2 tbsp sesame oil
4 tbsp teriyaki marinade
olive oil, for brushing
vegetable oil, for frying

100g/4oz sliced pickled ginger,
  drained and dried
4 garlic cloves, peeled and thinly
  sliced
4-6 spring onions, thinly sliced

**1** Trim the beef of any fat or sinew, then place in a non-metallic dish. Spoon
the sesame oil and teriyaki marinade over the meat and turn to coat well.
Cover and leave to marinate in the fridge for at least 4 hours, preferably
overnight, turning the meat occasionally.

**2** Bring to room temperature, lift the meat out of the marinade and pat dry.

**3** Preheat grill to high. Brush meat sparingly with olive oil and sear all over
under the grill for 2 minutes, turning as necessary. Turn down the heat to
medium and grill for a further 20 minutes, turning 3 times.

**4** Transfer the meat to a warm dish, cover with foil and leave to rest in a
warm place for 10 minutes.

**5** Meanwhile, heat a 1cm/½in depth of oil in a frying pan until a small piece
of bread sizzles instantly as it touches the oil. Add the ginger, sliced garlic
and spring onions and fry until golden. Remove with a slotted spoon and
drain on kitchen paper.

**6** Serve the meat thinly sliced, drizzled with the meat juices and scattered
with the ginger, garlic and spring onions.

This marinated, grilled fillet of beef is dark
on the outside, but remains pink and moist
inside. It is served with frazzled pickled
ginger, spring onions and garlic.

# Savoy cabbage and veal parcels

illustrated on previous pages

**Serves 2**

6 medium green Savoy cabbage
leaves
2 tsp olive oil
2 shallots, finely chopped
1 garlic clove, crushed
280g/10oz lean minced veal

1 tsp finely chopped fresh
rosemary leaves
4 juniper berries, crushed
150ml/¼ pint well flavoured
chicken stock
50g/2oz fresh breadcrumbs
salt and pepper

**1** Blanch the cabbage leaves in boiling water for 1-2 minutes. Drain and refresh in cold water, then drain and leave to dry on kitchen paper while preparing the filling.

**2** Heat the oil in a pan and fry the shallots and garlic for 5 minutes or until soft and translucent. Add the minced veal with the rosemary and crushed juniper berries; fry for 5-6 minutes until opaque. Add the stock and continue cooking for 2-3 minutes.

**3** Remove from the heat and add the breadcrumbs. Mix thoroughly, seasoning with pepper and a little salt if required.

**4** Divide the veal mixture between the cabbage leaves. Fold in the sides of the leaves, then roll up loosely from the stem end. Secure each parcel with a wooden cocktail stick.

**5** Put the cabbage parcels in a steamer and steam for 8-10 minutes until the cabbage is tender and the filling is piping hot. Serve with a fresh tomato sauce.

**Note** Use pork instead of veal for the filling. To keep the fat content low, buy lean pork fillet (tenderloin) and mince it yourself.

Cabbage leaves envelop a tasty veal stuffing flavoured with shallots, rosemary and juniper – perfect with a fresh tomato sauce.

# Mediterranean veal rolls

2 large veal escalopes, each about
175g/6oz
**For the stuffing**
50g packet sun-dried aubergine
slices
2 canned or bottled red peppers
(capsicums), drained

olive oil, for brushing
salt and pepper
1 buffalo mozzarella cheese, about
150g/5oz, sliced
handful of fresh basil leaves

**1** For the stuffing, soak the aubergine slices in tepid water for 20 minutes.
Drain and pat dry with kitchen paper.
**2** Put the veal escalopes between sheets of greaseproof paper and bat out
thinly, without tearing the meat.
**3** Lay the peppers on top of each escalope, followed by the aubergines. Brush
with olive oil, season with salt and pepper, then cover with the sliced
mozzarella and basil leaves.
**4** Preheat grill to medium. Roll the veal escalopes up from the longest side,
enclosing the filling. Secure with cocktail sticks and brush with olive oil.
Grill for 20 minutes, gradually turning the parcels to ensure even cooking.
**5** Serve cut into slices, with a salad.

**Note** To barbecue, cook the veal parcels over medium coals for 15-20 minutes,
turning from time to time.

Flattened veal escalopes rolled around a tasty
stuffing of mozzarella, capsicums, sun-dried
aubergine and basil.

# Venison in coppa with chestnuts

**Serves 4-6**

1 tsp black mustard seeds
1 tsp juniper berries
1 tsp black peppercorns
600g/1lb 5oz piece venison fillet
salt
350g/12oz shelled fresh chestnuts
   (in skins)

1 tbsp oil
115g/4oz coppa (20 thin slices),
   or pancetta
100ml/3½fl oz fruity red wine
knob of unsalted butter

**1** Coarsely grind the mustard seeds, juniper and peppercorns, with a pestle and mortar. Rub the mixture all over the venison. Wrap tightly in cling film; refrigerate for 24 hours.

**2** Bring the meat to room temperature 1 hour before cooking and season lightly with salt. Preheat oven to 220C/fan oven 200C/Gas 7.

**3** Pierce the skin of each chestnut, then put in a shallow roasting dish and toss with the oil. Season with salt and roast for 5 minutes.

**4** Lay the coppa slices overlapping on greaseproof paper to form a rectangle, large enough to wrap around the venison. Lay the venison on the long edge and, with the aid of the paper, roll the coppa around it to enclose. Wrap in oiled foil and roast with the chestnuts for 15 minutes.

**5** Unwrap the venison, pour the juices into a small pan, then roast for a further 5 minutes until the coppa is slightly crisp. Transfer to a serving dish, cover loosely and rest in a warm place for 15 minutes; continue to roast the chestnuts during this time.

**6** Add the wine to the meat juices and boil for 1 minute. Stir in the butter. Carve the meat and serve with the chestnuts and glaze.

Venison is marinated overnight with juniper and mustard, then wrapped in coppa and roasted with chestnuts.

# Mahogany duck breasts with fruity salsa

4 duck breasts, each 175-200g/6-7oz
salt and pepper
**For the salsa**
1 small dessert apple

2 slices fresh pineapple
2 tbsp dried cranberries
finely grated rind and juice of
  ½ lemon, or to taste

**1** Pat the duck breasts dry with kitchen paper. Score the fat in a criss-cross pattern and rub with plenty of salt. Set aside.

**2** Core and finely dice the apple. Finely dice the pineapple and mix with the cranberries and apple. Add lemon juice and rind to taste, and season with salt and pepper.

**3** Preheat grill to medium. Place the duck breasts, skin side down, on the grill rack and grill for 1 minute to sear the underside.

**4** Turn the duck breasts over and grill under the medium heat for 10 minutes. Reduce the heat to low and continue to cook for a further 10 minutes until the skin is dark brown; the flesh should be just rosy pink.

**5** Slice the duck breasts and serve accompanied by the fruity salsa.

**Note** To barbecue, cook the duck breasts flesh side down for 1 minute to seal. Turn over and cook for 10 minutes, dowsing any flames with water as the fat can catch and ignite. Lift the barbecue rack away from the heat source a little and continue to cook for a further 10 minutes.

Duck breasts are grilled slowly until the skin is mahogany brown, then served with a zesty salsa of apple, pineapple, dried cranberries and lemon.

# Duck with caramelised orange and Campari

1 Gressingham duck, about 1.8kg/4lb
200g/7oz sugar
juice of 1 orange
3 tbsp Campari
1 small onion, peeled

5 large fresh rosemary sprigs
salt
1 small orange, cut into slices
150ml/¼ pint well flavoured duck
   or chicken stock

**1** Sit the duck on a rack in the sink and pour over 2 kettlefuls of boiling water. Drain and let dry on kitchen paper in a cool place for 30 minutes, or hang the duck so air can circulate around it. (This firms up the skin.)
**2** Preheat oven to 220C/fan oven 200C/Gas 7. Put the sugar, orange juice and 2 tbsp Campari in a heavy based pan on a low heat until the sugar is dissolved. Bring to the boil and simmer for 5 minutes or until syrupy.
**3** Prick the duck skin all over. Put the onion and 1 rosemary sprig into the cavity. Sit the duck on a rack in a roasting tin containing 150ml/¼ pint water. Roast for 20 minutes.
**4** Brush the duck with some of the syrup and sprinkle with salt. Roast for a further 30 minutes. Brush with more syrup and roast for another 30 minutes, lowering the setting to 200C/fan oven 180C/Gas 6 if the duck appears to be overbrowning.
**5** Dip the orange slices in the remaining syrup and lay on the duck breast with the rosemary sprigs. Brush all over with the syrup and roast for a final 30 minutes or until the duck is cooked.
**6** Transfer to a platter, cover loosely and rest in a warm place for 15 minutes. Pour off fat from roasting tin, then place over a medium heat. Add stock and remaining Campari, stirring to deglaze. Add any remaining syrup and heat through. Serve with the duck.

# Barbecued lamb with salmoriglio sauce

**Serves 4-6**
2 racks of lamb, each with
  6-7 cutlets
salt and pepper
olive oil, for brushing

**For the salmoriglio sauce**
175ml/6fl oz extra virgin olive oil
juice of 1 large or 2 small lemons
2 tsp dried oregano
2 garlic cloves, finely chopped
2 tbsp chopped fresh parsley

**1** Trim the lamb racks of excess fat, but retain a thin covering to keep the meat moist during cooking. Rub all over with salt and pepper and lightly brush with olive oil.

**2** To make the sauce, whisk all of the ingredients together in a bowl until well combined and thick.

**3** Preheat grill to medium. Lay the racks of lamb down, fat side up, in the grill pan and grill for 15-20 minutes, checking frequently to make sure that the fat doesn't catch.

**4** As soon as the meat is cooked, transfer to a warmed dish and pour over the sauce. Cover and leave to rest in a warm place for 10 minutes. Serve the lamb, cut into double cutlets, with the sauce spooned over.

**Note** Dried oregano is preferred to fresh here, for its intense, sweet flavour.

Racks of lamb are grilled to perfection, then drenched in a Sicilian sauce of lemon, garlic, oregano and olive oil – to bring all the scents of southern Italy to your kitchen.

# Loin of lamb with mushrooms and nuts

700-900g/1½-2lb boned loin of lamb
salt and pepper
1 tbsp olive oil
2 shallots, finely chopped
1 garlic clove, crushed
150g/5½oz chestnut mushrooms, diced
1 small celery stick, finely chopped

100g/4oz cooked, peeled chestnuts (fresh or vacuum packed), roughly chopped
1 tsp paprika
85g/3oz walnuts, finely chopped
25g/1oz fresh breadcrumbs
2 tbsp vin de noix (walnut aperitif) or dry sherry

**1** Cut away any skin and excess fat from the joint, leaving a thin coating. Score this in a criss cross pattern and rub with seasoning.
**2** For the stuffing, heat the oil in a pan and fry the shallots and garlic until transparent. Add the mushrooms and cook gently until softened and all moisture is evaporated.
**3** Add the celery, chestnuts and paprika and cook for 2-3 minutes, then add the walnuts, breadcrumbs, aperitif and 1 tbsp water. Season to taste and let cool slightly. Preheat oven to 190C/fan oven 170C/Gas 5.
**4** Turn the meat flesh side up, and spread with the stuffing. Roll up and tie with string at 2.5cm/1in intervals. Place on a trivet in a roasting tin and roast for 1¼-1½ hours, or 2 hours for well done meat.
**5** Leave the lamb to rest in a warm place for 10 minutes before carving.

A tasty chestnut and mushroom stuffing accentuates the sweet taste of the lamb.

# Lamb with Chinese spices

2 tsp sunflower oil
500g/1lb 2oz lean lamb fillet, cut
  into chunks
1 tbsp fresh root ginger julienne
  (fine sticks)
1 tsp Chinese five spice powder
4 tbsp Chinese rice wine or dry
  sherry

4 tbsp dark soy sauce
3 tbsp clear honey
227g can water chestnuts, drained
2 leeks, sliced on the diagonal
1 large red pepper, cored, seeded and
  cut into diamonds
shredded spring onion, to garnish
  (optional)

**1** Heat the oil in a large heavy-based pan or flameproof casserole. Add the lamb and ginger and stir-fry until the meat is evenly coloured. Sprinkle with the five spice powder, then stir in the wine or sherry, soy sauce, honey and water chestnuts. Bring to a simmer.

**2** Cover the pan with a tight fitting lid and simmer over a gentle heat for 20 minutes.

**3** Stir in the leeks and red pepper, then cover and cook for a further 40 minutes until the meat and vegetables are tender.

**4** If preparing ahead, cool, cover and refrigerate for up to 2 days, or freeze.

**5** To serve, defrost at cool room temperature overnight (if frozen). Reheat in a pan until piping hot.

**6** Serve topped with shredded spring onion if wished. Accompany with rice, or noodles tossed with bean sprouts and steamed shredded sugar snaps.

**Variation** Replace the water chestnuts with a 227g can sliced bamboo shoots. Serve sprinkled with toasted cashew nuts.

Rich soy sauce, honey and the star anise in Chinese five spice powder add intriguing flavours to this casserole.

# Lamb stuffed with dates and spices

8 tbsp olive oil

2 onions, 1 chopped, 1 finely sliced

2 plump garlic cloves, 1 crushed,
  1 cut into slivers

large pinch of saffron strands

¼ tsp ground cinnamon

1 tsp ground cumin

salt and pepper

8 medjool dates, stoned and finely
  chopped

2 pieces preserved lemon, rinsed
  and finely chopped, or finely
  grated rind of 2 lemons

3-4 tbsp chopped fresh coriander
  leaves

1.3kg/3lb leg of lamb, part boned
  (see note)

2 cinnamon sticks, broken

**1** Heat 4 tbsp oil in a heavy based frying pan and fry the chopped onion and crushed garlic until soft and golden. Add the saffron, cinnamon, cumin and seasoning; stir well. Take off the heat and add the dates and lemon. Stir to mix and set aside until cold.

**2** Mix the fresh coriander into the stuffing and use to stuff the lamb. Secure with skewers or sew up the stuffed pocket.

**3** Preheat oven to 200C/fan oven 180C/Gas 6. Make small incisions in the skin of the lamb and insert the garlic slivers. Put in a roasting tin and brush with 2 tbsp oil. Season well and surround with the cinnamon sticks.

**4** Roast for 1 hour 20 minutes, basting from time to time. Transfer to a warm platter, cover loosely and rest in a warm place for 15 minutes. Meanwhile, fry the sliced onion in the remaining oil until golden and crisp.

**5** Serve the lamb topped with the fried onion and cinnamon sticks.

**Note** Part boning leg of lamb to give a pocket for the stuffing is not difficult. Given notice, your butcher should to do it for you.

# Thai-style lamb shanks

4 lamb shanks
1 tbsp vegetable oil
2 large onions, finely chopped
2 tbsp Thai green curry paste
2 tbsp lemon grass, finely chopped
1 tsp ground cumin
1 tsp ground coriander

400ml can coconut milk
500ml/18fl oz vegetable stock
3 tbsp chopped fresh coriander leaves
salt and pepper
**To garnish**
coriander leaves or finely sliced chilli

**1** Preheat oven to 220C/fan oven 200C/Gas 7. Place the lamb shanks in a roasting tin and roast for 40 minutes, turning them halfway through cooking.

**2** Lift out the lamb shanks, drain off all of the fat, then transfer to a casserole in which they fit snugly. Lower the oven setting to 190C/fan oven 170C/Gas 5.

**3** Heat the oil in another pan, add the onions and sauté until light golden. Add the curry paste, lemon grass, cumin and coriander and stir-fry for 1 minute. Add the coconut milk, stock and chopped coriander.

**4** Pour this mixture over the lamb shanks, cover and cook in the oven for 2½ hours until the meat is very tender. Check the seasoning of the sauce.

**5** To serve, place each lamb shank in a warmed shallow serving bowl. Spoon over some of the sauce and scatter with fresh coriander or sliced chilli. Serve with Thai jasmine rice and a steamed green vegetable, such as bok choi.

These succulent shanks of lamb are subtly flavoured with coconut milk and Thai spices and baked until meltingly tender.

# Baked aubergines with minted lamb

4 aubergines, each about 225g/8oz
280g/10oz thin cut lean lamb fillet
salt and pepper
1 red onion, thinly sliced
2 tbsp shredded fresh mint leaves
a little oil, for brushing (optional)

**For the minted yogurt**
200ml/7fl oz low fat yogurt
1-2 tbsp finely shredded fresh mint
1 garlic clove, crushed (optional)

**1** Preheat a baking tray in the oven at 200C/fan oven 180C/Gas 6. Cut each aubergine lengthwise into 5 slices, but not quite right through.
**2** Season the lamb with salt and pepper and insert a slice into each aubergine slit, with some onion and shredded mint. Brush sparingly with oil and loosely wrap each aubergine in foil.
**3** Place the parcels on the baking tray and bake for 45 minutes to 1 hour until the aubergine is tender through to the centre.
**4** Meanwhile, mix the yogurt with the mint, salt, and garlic if using. Chill until required.
**5** Serve the baked aubergines hot, accompanied by the minted yogurt and basmati rice or steamed couscous.

Tasty aubergines are slit and filled with slices of lean lamb fillet and aromatic flavourings, then baked to perfection. Minted, garlicky yogurt is the ideal complement.

# Rabbit in wine with olives and oregano

800g/1¾lb boneless rabbit portions, cut into large chunks
4 tbsp seasoned flour
2-3 tbsp olive oil
250g/9oz large shallots, peeled and quartered
2 large garlic cloves, crushed

250g/9oz large button mushrooms, halved
300ml/½ pint dry white wine
150ml/¼ pint chicken stock
100g/4oz green olives
2 tbsp chopped fresh oregano
salt and pepper

**1** Coat the rabbit pieces in the seasoned flour. Heat the oil in a flameproof casserole and fry the rabbit in batches until golden on all sides; remove with a slotted spoon. Add the shallots, garlic and mushrooms to the pan; stir-fry for 3 minutes.

**2** Pour in the wine and stock, return the rabbit pieces and stir in the olives and oregano. Cover tightly and simmer for about 30 minutes until the rabbit is tender. Taste and adjust the seasoning.

**3** If preparing ahead, cool, cover and refrigerate for up to 2 days.

**4** To serve, reheat in a flameproof casserole or heavy based pan until piping hot. Serve with creamy mashed potatoes and a green vegetable.

Make this delicious wine-enriched casserole in advance to allow time for the flavours to fully develop.

# Jamaican jerk pork chops

4 spring onions, finely chopped
2 red chillies, seeded and chopped
3 tbsp vegetable oil
1 tsp allspice
2 tbsp light muscovado sugar

2 tbsp vinegar
2 tsp fresh thyme leaves
salt and pepper
4 pork loin chops, each about
  200g/7oz

**1** Put the spring onions, chillies, oil, allspice, sugar, vinegar and thyme leaves in a food processor. Season well and process until well blended.

**2** Make 3-4 shallow slashes on both sides of each pork chop and lay in a shallow, non-metallic dish. Pour the jerk mixture over the chops and turn them to coat thoroughly. Cover and then leave to marinate in a cool place for 1 hour.

**3** Preheat the grill to medium high. Transfer the chops to the grill rack and grill for 5-7 minutes on each side or until the meat is tender, basting them occasionally.

**4** Serve the grilled chops accompanied by baked sweet potatoes and an avocado, tomato and red onion salad.

This traditional Jamaican recipe, usually made with chicken-on-the-bone, works well with pork chops too. It is also a great recipe for a barbecue.

# Crisp roast stuffed shoulder of pork

**Serves 4-6**

1.3kg/3lb joint boneless shoulder of
  pork, with scored rind
100g/4oz pitted Agen prunes

4 tbsp Calvados or Marsala
grated rind and juice of 1 orange
sea salt and pepper
1 tsp clear honey

**1** Soak the prunes in the Calvados for 3-4 hours. Drain, reserving the liquor.
**2** Preheat oven to 220C/fan oven 200C/Gas 7. Open out the rolled joint of
pork and rub about 2 tsp sea salt into the slits of the scored rind.
**3** Turn the joint over, spoon the prunes on to the flesh and sprinkle with
the orange rind.
**4** Roll up the meat and secure with string, tied at 2.5cm/1in intervals.
Put the meat in a roasting tin and add 4 tbsp water to prevent the fat
spluttering. Roast for about 20 minutes until the crackling is formed.
**5** Reduce oven setting to 180C/fan oven 160C/Gas 4. Roast for a further
1½ hours, adding a little more water as needed.
**6** Lift the meat on to a warm serving dish and rest in a warm place for
10 minutes. Skim off the fat from the roasting juices, then add the reserved
Calvados, orange juice and honey. Stir to scrape up the sediment and boil
to reduce slightly, to a glaze; season.
**7** Carve the pork into thick slices and serve with the meat glaze.

Succulent roast pork flavoured with juicy
Agen prunes and a hint of Calvados. To ensure
a crisp crackling, make sure the pork rind
is deeply scored.

# Pork and rosemary skewers

450g/1lb pork fillet
4 fresh rosemary sprigs, leaves only
3 tbsp balsamic vinegar
2 tbsp sun-dried tomato paste

4 tbsp olive oil
salt and pepper
lime wedges, to serve

**1** Pre-soak 8 wooden kebab skewers in cold water for 20 minutes.
**2** Trim the pork of any membrane, then cut lengthways into 16 thin strips.
**3** Pound the rosemary leaves with the balsamic vinegar, sun-dried tomato
paste, olive oil, salt and pepper, using a pestle and mortar. Transfer to a
dish. Add the pork strips and turn to coat. Cover and leave to marinate in
the fridge for at least 1 hour.
**4** Preheat grill to high. Thread 2 pork strips in a zig-zag fashion on to each
of the skewers. Lay on a foil-lined grill pan and grill for 2-3 minutes each
side, or until browned on all sides and cooked through.
**5** Serve with lime wedges, and a salad.

**Variation** Use stripped rosemary branches for the kebab skewers. Strip
the leaves from 8 woody stems, leaving about 2.5cm/1in intact at one end.
Thread the pork on to the stems and grill as above.

**Note** To barbecue, cook over hot coals for about 2 minutes per side.

Strips of pork fillet are marinated in crushed
rosemary, balsamic vinegar and sun-dried
tomato paste, then threaded zig-zag fashion
on to skewers and grilled.

# Crusted roast loin of pork

Illustrated on previous pages

**Serves 6-8**

1.3kg/3lb loin of pork, with 6-8 bones (see note)

1 tbsp balsamic vinegar

4 tsp caraway seeds, roughly crushed

2 tsp white peppercorns, roughly crushed

3 tsp Malden salt

9 sprigs of fresh bay leaves

2 tbsp olive oil

**1** Tie the meat with string to ensure the bones stand upright. Rub well with balsamic vinegar and leave to stand for 20 minutes. Preheat oven to 200C/fan oven 180C/Gas 6.

**2** Mix caraway, white pepper and salt together and press over the meat. Lay 1 bay sprig in a shallow roasting tin. Stand the pork loin on top and drizzle with the oil. Roast for 15 minutes, basting with the pan juices occasionally.

**3** Push the rest of the bay leaf sprigs under the string and roast for a further 20 minutes.

**4** Lower oven setting to 180C/fan oven 160C/ Gas 4. Cover the meat loosely with foil and roast for a further 30 minutes or until cooked through. To test, insert a skewer into the middle: the juices should run clear.

**5** Lift meat on to a dish, cover loosely and rest in a warm place for 15 minutes. Meanwhile, pour off the fat from the tin, then add 3 tbsp water, stirring to deglaze.

**6** Scatter the loin with the remaining salt and serve cut into thick slices with the bone attached, and the pan juices spooned over. Serve with baked baby beets and potatoes.

**Note** Buy a whole pork loin with 6-8 chops and ask your butcher to remove all skin, fat and connecting bone, leaving the thin individual bone attached to each chop.

# Pork steaks with sloe gin

4 pork leg steaks, trimmed of fat
2 tbsp well seasoned flour
25g/1oz butter
4 juniper berries, finely chopped
100ml/3½fl oz sloe gin

150ml/¼ pint double cream
1 tbsp finely chopped fresh flat
 leaf parsley
salt and pepper

**1** Toss the pork steaks in the seasoned flour to coat lightly on both sides, shaking off excess.
**2** Melt the butter in a large frying pan and scatter in the juniper berries. Add the pork steaks and fry for about 3 minutes each side until just cooked through and turning golden.
**3** Pour in the sloe gin and allow to bubble until reduced by half.
**4** Lift out the pork steaks and transfer to hot serving plates; keep warm. Add the cream to the pan juices with the chopped parsley and stir to make a sauce, scraping up any sediment from the base of the pan. Season with salt and pepper to taste. Bring to a simmer, stirring.
**5** Pour this sauce over the pork steaks and serve at once with new potatoes, broccoli and sugar snaps.

**Note** Sloe gin is available from selected supermarkets and off licences. Alternatively you can, of course, make your own in the autumn by macerating sloes, picked from the hedgerows, with gin and sugar.

Pork steaks are cooked with a hint of juniper, then served in a rich creamy, sloe gin sauce for a special supper.

# Chilli pork and cheese burgers

750g/1lb 10oz minced pork
2 garlic cloves, crushed
2 tbsp sweet chilli sauce
3 spring onions, finely chopped
3 tbsp chopped fresh coriander
   leaves

salt and pepper
50g/2oz gorgonzola cheese
oil, for brushing
**To serve**
4 muffins or burger buns, split
   and toasted

**1** Put the minced pork, garlic, chilli sauce, spring onions and chopped coriander in a bowl. Season with salt and pepper and mix thoroughly until the mixture holds together, Divide into 4 equal portions and then shape into flat cakes.

**2** Cut the blue cheese into 4 cubes and mould each portion of pork mixture around a cheese cube to enclose. Flatten to form fat burgers.

**3** Preheat grill to medium. Brush the pork burgers with a little oil. Place on the grill rack and cook under the medium grill for about 7 minutes each side until cooked through. (Alternatively, you can barbecue the burgers over medium hot coals allowing about 6 minutes per side.)

**4** Serve at once, on toasted muffins or burger buns, with chips, ketchup and mustard if you like.

**Note** Bring meat to room temperature before grilling, and preheat the grill for at least 10 minutes. Temperature settings of grills vary considerably, so treat suggested cooking times as guidelines only. if you are barbecuing rather than grilling, remember to light the coals well ahead and wait until they are 'white hot' before starting to cook. Always test meat to ensure it is properly cooked to your liking.

These spicy burgers reveal a hidden pocket of melted blue cheese when cut open.

# Sausage and apple pie with potato crust

**For the pastry**
225g/8oz self-raising flour
¼ tsp salt
¼ tsp pepper
175g/6oz butter, diced
225g/8oz cold mashed potato
**For the filling**
1 tbsp olive oil
2 onions, chopped

2 cooking apples, about 350g/12oz, peeled, cored and chopped
900g/2lb low fat pork sausages, skinned
195g can sweetcorn, drained
¼ tsp grated fresh nutmeg
½ tsp ground black pepper
½ tsp salt
1 large egg, beaten

**1** For the pastry, sift the flour and seasoning into a bowl, then rub in the butter until the mixture resembles breadcrumbs. Add the potato and work to a soft dough. Wrap in cling film and chill while making the filling.
**2** Heat the oil in a pan and fry the onions until beginning to soften. Add the apples and cook, stirring occasionally, for 2-3 minutes until starting to soften, then turn into a bowl.
**3** Add the sausagemeat, sweetcorn, nutmeg, seasoning and beaten egg. Mix thoroughly with clean hands and then transfer to a shallow 1.4 litre/2½ pint pie dish.
**4** Lightly press out the pastry with your hands on a lightly floured surface until large enough to cover the pie. Carefully lift over the filling, trim the edges and make a slit in the top of the pie. Chill for up to 24 hours until ready to bake.
**5** Preheat a baking tray in the oven at 190C/fan oven 170C/Gas 5. Place the pie on the baking tray and bake for 1-1¼ hours, covering lightly with foil if the pastry appears to be overbrowning. Serve hot, with seasonal vegetables.

This potato pastry has a lovely light, buttery texture. For best results, use low fat sausages for the filling.

# Maple and mustard glazed ham

**Serves 6-8**

1 bone-in ham, smoked or
   unsmoked, about 3kg/6½lb
   (see note)

150ml/¼ pint maple syrup
25g/1oz caster sugar
2 tsp Dijon or honey mustard
15 cloves

**1** Preheat oven to 180C/fan oven 160C/Gas 4. Line a large roasting tin
with a sheet of extra wide foil, allowing plenty of overhang at each end.
Lay another sheet of foil crosswise on top, to overhang the sides of the tin
generously. Put the ham in the centre and bring the ends of the foil up over
the top. Fold together to seal well and make a roomy tent over the ham.
Bake in the oven, allowing 30 minutes per 450g/1lb.
**2** Put the maple syrup and sugar in a small heavy based pan and heat gently
until the sugar is dissolved. Add the mustard and simmer until syrupy.
**3** Drain off the juices from the ham. Increase oven setting to 220C/fan oven
200C/Gas 7. Cut a zig zag pattern in the skin at the narrow end of the joint,
to about 7.5cm/3in from the end. Remove the skin from the rest of the ham,
leaving a layer of fat. Score the fat in a lattice pattern, at 2.5cm/1in intervals.
**4** Brush the whole joint with half of the syrup. Roast, uncovered, for
5 minutes per 450g/1lb until glazed and golden, brushing with the
remaining syrup and studding each lattice with a clove halfway through
this time.
**5** If serving hot, allow to rest in a warm place for 20 minutes; if serving
cold, leave to cool completely.

**Note** Ask your butcher for the knuckle end to get a traditional ham shape.
Unless it is mild cure or pre-soaked, you will need to soak it for 24 hours
before cooking otherwise the meat will be too salty.

This traditional whole baked ham is equally
good served hot with creamy mash and peas
or cold with salads.

# smart
# vegetables
# and salads

# Caramelised leeks on sweet potato rösti

1 kg/2¼lb sweet potatoes
1 egg, beaten
4 tbsp olive oil
25g/1oz butter
300g/10oz shallots, peeled and split
250g/9oz baby leeks, halved

1 tsp finely chopped fresh sage
 leaves
1½ tsp sugar
salt and pepper
1 tbsp marsala (optional)
sage leaves, to garnish

**1** Preheat oven to 190C/fan oven 170C/Gas 5. Coarsely grate the sweet potatoes, mix with the beaten egg and season well. Shape the grated potato into 12 heaped spoonfuls on 2 oiled baking sheets, spacing apart. Flatten slightly and bake for 5-8 minutes until golden. Turn over and bake for a further 5 minutes.

**2** Heat 2 tbsp oil and half of the butter in a heavy based pan over a high heat until sizzling. Add the shallots, lower the heat, cover and cook for about 8 minutes until soft and evenly browned. Remove with a slotted spoon and place in a warm dish.

**3** Heat the remaining oil and butter in the pan over a high heat until sizzling. Add the leeks with the chopped sage and cook in the same way, for about 5 minutes.

**4** Increase heat and return shallots to the pan. Add the sugar, seasoning and marsala if using and cook, stirring, until caramelised. Arrange the röstis and vegetables on warmed plates, allowing 3 röstis per person. Serve at once, garnished with sage.

**Note** For convenience, you can prepare the röstis in advance. Reheat in oven at 200C/fan oven 180C/Gas 6 for 10 minutes to serve.

These tasty rosti are an ideal light main course for vegetarian entertaining.

# Thai mushroom and mangetout salad

Illustrated on previous pages

300g/10oz mangetout, halved
3 tbsp vegetable oil
2 garlic cloves, finely chopped
4 shallots, finely chopped
500g/1lb 2oz portobello mushrooms,
  stalks removed, thickly sliced
2 tsp clear honey
juice of 2 limes
2 tsp Thai fish sauce

2 tsp lemon grass, very finely
  chopped
1 hot red chilli (eg. bird's eye),
  finely sliced
3 tbsp fresh basil leaves, roughly
  torn
3 tbsp fresh coriander leaves,
  roughly torn
salt and pepper

**1** Cook the mangetout in boiling water for 2 minutes until just tender.
Drain and set aside.
**2** Heat the oil in a wok and stir-fry the garlic and shallots for 2 minutes.
Add the mushrooms and stir-fry for 5 minutes. Add the mangetout and
stir-fry for 1 minute. Turn into a bowl.
**3** Mix the honey, lime juice, fish sauce and lemon grass together, then add
to the salad with the chilli and herbs. Toss well and check the seasoning.
Serve the salad at room temperature.

**Note** Large flat mushrooms can be used instead of portobello mushrooms.

A delicious salad fragrantly flavoured with
lemon grass, chilli and lime juice.

# Pan fried feta cheese salad

6 tbsp instant polenta
1 tsp ground cumin
450g/1lb feta cheese, cut into
   12 slices
2 eggs, beaten
8 tbsp olive oil
2 Little Gem lettuce, separated
   into leaves
4 vine ripened tomatoes, sliced

1 large avocado, peeled, stoned
   and sliced
2 shallots, thinly sliced
**For the dressing**
1 large garlic clove, finely chopped
juice of 2 limes
4 tbsp clear honey (preferably acacia)
2 tbsp chopped fresh mint

**1** Mix polenta with cumin. Dip the feta slices in the egg, then coat in the spiced polenta.
**2** Heat half the oil in a large frying pan and fry the feta in batches on both sides until crisp.
**3** Meanwhile, mix the dressing ingredients with the remaining oil and 2 tbsp water.
**4** Pile the lettuce, tomatoes, avocado and shallot into bowls and top with the fried feta.
**5** Wipe any polenta from the pan, then pour in the dressing and heat until bubbling. Pour over the salad and serve, with warm pittas.

Hot feta slices with a crisp spicy coating, atop a tomato and avocado salad makes a delicious main course salad.

# Sri Lankan vegetable curry

500g/1lb 2oz pumpkin, peeled
   and seeded
225g/8oz potato, peeled
2 tbsp vegetable oil
1 onion, finely chopped
1-2 cinnamon sticks
2 garlic cloves, finely chopped
2 green chillies, seeded and
   finely sliced

¼ tsp turmeric
1 tsp fenugreek seeds
100g/4oz green beans, trimmed
   and halved
8-10 fresh curry leaves
400ml can coconut milk
salt and pepper

**1** Cut the pumpkin and potato into 2.5cm/1in cubes. Heat the oil in a large pan and gently fry the onion with the cinnamon until soft.
**2** Add the garlic, chillies, turmeric and fenugreek seeds. Cook, stirring, for 1 minute.
**3** Add the pumpkin, potato and green beans and fry, stirring, for 1-2 minutes. Add the curry leaves, coconut milk and 150ml/¼ pint water.
**4** Bring to the boil, then lower the heat and simmer, covered, for about 15 minutes. Season to taste and serve with rice.

A coconut based curry with pumpkin, potatoes and green beans, flavoured with fenugreek seeds and curry leaves.

# Grilled aubergine terrine

Illustrated on previous pages

2 large aubergines, about 700g/1lb
   9oz in total
6-8 tbsp extra virgin olive oil
salt and pepper
4 plum tomatoes, cored and cut into
   3mm/⅛in slices
135g jar black olive tapenade

18 fresh large basil leaves
   (about 20g/¾oz), stalks removed
**For the vinaigrette dressing**
2 tsp cider vinegar
2 tbsp olive oil
½ tsp Dijon mustard

**1** Cut the aubergines into 3mm/⅛in slices. Preheat the grill to high. Brush the aubergine slices with oil and season with salt and pepper. Grill in batches for 3-4 minutes each side or until golden, turning once. Drain on kitchen paper.

**2** Line the base and sides of a 450g/1lb non stick loaf tin with overlapping slices of aubergine. (Or use an ordinary loaf tin lined with cling film.)

**3** Arrange a layer of tomato slices in the tin. Spread a third of the tapenade over the tomato, then scatter over a third of the basil leaves. Cover with a layer of aubergine slices. Repeat these layers twice more, finally finishing with a layer of aubergine. Cover the terrine with cling film and chill in the refrigerator for 2-4 hours.

**4** For the dressing, put the ingredients in a screw topped jar, season with salt and pepper and shake well to emulsify.

**5** To serve, unmould the terrine on to a board or plate and cut into thick slices. Serve drizzled with the dressing.

Serve this elegant terrine as a stylish vegetarian lunch with toasted olive ciabatta.

# Spinach, ricotta and pistachio filo pie

**Serves 6**
8 large sheets filo pastry
**For the filling**
450g/1lb small, young spinach
  leaves
250g/9oz ricotta cheese, drained
100g/4oz shelled pistachio nuts,
  finely chopped
50g/2oz sun dried tomatoes, finely
  chopped

2 tbsp finely chopped fresh
  marjoram (optional)
salt and pepper
1 egg yolk, beaten
**To assemble**
1 egg white, beaten
85g/3oz butter, melted

**1** Grease a 25cm/10in springform cake tin or pizza tin.

**2** For the filling, blanch the spinach in boiling water for 30 seconds. Drain, refresh in cold water and drain well, squeezing out as much moisture as possible. Chop the spinach finely and place in a bowl.

**3** Add the ricotta, pistachio nuts, sun dried tomatoes, and marjoram if using. Mix well and season, then stir in the egg yolk to bind the mixture.

**4** Preheat oven to 220C/fan oven 200C/Gas 7. Lay one sheet of filo on a clean surface; keep the rest wrapped to prevent it drying. Take an eighth of the filling and lay it along one long edge of the filo. Roll up to within 1cm/½in from the edge, to form a lip (for the next roll to sit on).

**5** Curl the roll into a coil and place in the centre of the tin. Brush the lip with egg white, then brush the top of the filo roll with melted butter.

**6** Repeat with the rest of the filo and filling, positioning the rolls in the tin as you make them to form a continuous spiral. (The final roll will not need a lip.)

**7** Brush the top of the filo pie with the remaining butter and bake for 20-30 minutes until golden and crisp. Carefully unmould the pie onto a flat plate and serve hot or cold, with a salad.

Serve this unusual vegetarian filo pie either hot or cold, with a leafy salad.

# Goat's cheese and bacon gougère

4 rindless smoked streaky bacon
  rashers
115g/4oz butter
150ml/¼ pint water
115g/4oz strong plain flour
1 tsp English mustard
4 large eggs, beaten
salt and pepper
115g/4oz soft goat's cheese, in pieces

**For the filling**
3 tbsp olive oil
3 garlic cloves, crushed
450g/1lb courgettes, thickly sliced
1 large aubergine, cubed
400g can chopped tomatoes
1 tbsp chopped fresh oregano
1 tsp sugar
50g/2oz pitted green olives

**1** Preheat oven to 220C/fan oven 200C/Gas 7. Grease 4 individual
300ml/½ pint soufflé dishes. Dry-fry the bacon in a pan until crisp, then
snip into small pieces.
**2** To make the choux pastry, put the butter and water in a heavy based pan
and heat until the butter is melted and the mixture boils. Add the flour all
at once and beat vigorously over the heat for about 1 minute until the
mixture leaves the side of the pan. Take off the heat and stir until lukewarm.
**3** Add the mustard, then gradually beat in the eggs, until smooth. Stir
in the bacon and season. Carefully fold in the cheese, so that it forms
pockets through the mixture.
**4** Divide the mixture between the soufflé dishes and bake for 25 minutes
until well risen and golden.
**5** Meanwhile, prepare the filling. Heat the oil in a pan and fry the garlic,
courgettes and aubergine until beginning to soften. Stir in the tomatoes,
oregano, sugar and seasoning, Cover and simmer for 15 minutes.
**6** Add the olives to the vegetables. Spoon some on top of the gougère; serve
the remainder separately.

Goat's cheese and crisp fried smoked bacon
add a savoury tang to choux pastry. For a
vegetarian dish, omit the bacon.

# Roasted aubergine and red rice salad

Illustrated on previous pages

2 medium aubergines, 500g/1lb 2oz
in total
2 tbsp tahini paste
salt and pepper
1 tbsp sesame seeds
2 red onions, cut into wedges

1 tbsp olive oil
200g/7oz red Camargue rice
200g/7oz radicchio, torn
handful of rocket leaves
a little walnut oil and lemon juice
(optional)

**1** Preheat oven to 220C/fan oven 200C/Gas 7. Cut aubergines into 4cm/1½in cubes, brush with tahini and place in a non-stick roasting tin. Season and sprinkle with sesame seeds.

**2** Put the onion wedges in another roasting tin and sprinkle with olive oil.

**3** Put both tins in the oven and roast for about 40 minutes or until tender, swapping shelves halfway through cooking.

**4** Meanwhile, put the rice in a pan with 600ml/1 pint cold water. Bring to the boil, reduce heat, cover and simmer for about 40 minutes until tender. Drain if necessary.

**5** Allow the vegetables and rice to cool slightly, then gently toss together while still warm. Set aside to cool further.

**6** Serve warm or cold on the radicchio and rocket, dressed with a little walnut oil and lemon juice if liked.

A rustic dish of intriguing flavours and muted colours – delicious warm or cold – as a vegetarian main course.

# Gado gado

250g/9oz potatoes, halved if large
3 carrots, cut into 5mm/¼in slices
225g/8oz green beans, halved
250g/9oz white or Savoy cabbage,
  cored and thinly shredded
1 small cucumber, thickly sliced
200g/7oz bean sprouts
4 hard-boiled eggs, quartered
50g/2oz roasted peanuts, roughly
  chopped

**For the dressing**
1 tbsp vegetable oil
1 small onion, finely chopped
2 garlic cloves, finely chopped
1 red chilli, finely chopped
200g/7oz crunchy peanut butter
200ml/7fl oz coconut milk
150ml/¼ pint water
1 tbsp soy sauce
1 tbsp tomato ketchup

**1** Cook the potatoes in lightly salted water until just tender. Drain and leave until cool enough to handle, then peel and cut into 5mm/¼in slices.
**2** Add the carrots to a pan of boiling salted water and blanch for 5 minutes; drain and refresh in cold water; drain thoroughly. Repeat with the green beans and cabbage, allowing 3-5 minutes blanching time for the beans, 3 minutes for the cabbage.
**3** To make the dressing, heat the oil in a heavy based pan. Add the onion, garlic and chilli and cook gently for 5 minutes. Add the peanut butter, coconut milk and water. Bring to the boil, stirring constantly. Lower the heat, then add the soy sauce and tomato ketchup. Remove from the heat, stir well and leave to cool.
**4** Arrange all of the vegetables and the hard-boiled eggs on a large serving platter in separate piles. Scatter over the roasted peanuts.
**5** To serve, spoon some of the dressing over the eggs and vegetables. Serve the remainder separately.

This classic, substantial Indonesian salad is served with a creamy coconut and peanut dressing, spiked with garlic and chilli.

# Vegetable and goat's cheese salad

200g/7oz small, young leeks
140g/5oz sugar snap peas
280g/10oz asparagus
50g/2oz pumpkin seeds

140g/5oz firm goat's cheese,
  cubed pepper
a little walnut or olive oil,
  for drizzling

**1** Cut the leeks into 2.5cm/1in lengths, put into a steamer and steam for 2 minutes. Add the sugar snaps and cook for a further 5 minutes. Transfer both vegetables to a warm bowl; set aside.
**2** Cut the asparagus into 5cm/2in lengths and steam for 5 minutes or until just tender. Add to the other vegetables.
**3** Preheat a heavy based frying pan and dry fry the pumpkin seeds for 2 minutes until they begin to pop and brown slightly.
**4** Arrange the vegetables in a serving dish. Top with the goat's cheese, pumpkin seeds and pepper. Drizzle with a little walnut or olive oil and serve with warm, crusty bread as a light lunch or supper.

A delicious warm salad of asparagus, leeks and sugar snaps, topped with goat's cheese and toasted pumpkin seeds.

# Butternut risotto with rocket

4 tbsp pumpkin seeds
50g/2oz butter
2 onions, finely chopped
3 garlic cloves, thinly sliced
350g/12oz arborio or other
   risotto rice
1.2 litres/2 pints chicken or
   vegetable stock

1 butternut squash, about 550g/1lb
   4oz, peeled, seeded and cubed
150ml/¼ pint extra dry vermouth
100g/4oz pecorino or Parmesan
   shavings
25g/1oz rocket leaves
salt and pepper

**1** Dry fry the pumpkin seeds in a large frying pan for 1 minute until they start to pop. Remove and set aside.

**2** Melt the butter in the pan and fry the onions and garlic for 5 minutes to soften. Add the rice and stir to coat in the butter.

**3** Pour in the boiling stock and boil for 5 minutes, stirring frequently.

**4** Add the squash, vermouth and 300ml/½ pint boiling water. Return to the boil, lower heat and cook, stirring often, for 10 minutes until the rice and squash are just tender.

**5** Add two thirds of the cheese, half the rocket and the pumpkin seeds. Season to taste. Serve the risotto topped with the remaining rocket and cheese shavings.

**Note** For an authentic creamy texture, it is essential to use a risotto rice, such as arborio or carnaroli, rather than a long grain variety.

Butternut squash, toasted pumpkin seeds, peppery rocket leaves and pecorino cheese make this a satisfying vegetarian meal.

# Red pepper tagine with harissa

4 tbsp olive oil

4 red peppers, cored, seeded and
roughly chopped

3 red onions, chopped

4 garlic cloves, crushed

½ tsp ground cumin

½ tsp ground coriander

½ tsp paprika

two 400g cans chopped tomatoes

two 420g cans red kidney beans

4 celery sticks, sliced

1 tbsp harissa (see note)

1 tsp salt

3-4 tbsp chopped fresh coriander

3-4 tbsp chopped fresh mint

mint or coriander sprigs, to garnish

**1** Heat the oil in a large pan. Add the red peppers, onions and garlic, and fry, stirring, over a high heat until softened. Stir in the spices and cook, stirring, for about 30 seconds to release their flavour.

**2** Pour in the tomatoes. Drain the liquid from the kidney beans into the pan, then stir in the celery, harissa and salt. Cover and simmer for 15 minutes or until the celery is just tender.

**3** Stir in the kidney beans and heat through until simmering. If preparing ahead, allow to cool, then cover and chill for up to 2 days, or freeze.

**4** To serve, defrost at cool room temperature overnight (if frozen). Reheat the tagine in a large pan until bubbling and stir in the chopped coriander and mint. Serve on a bed of steamed couscous, garnished with mint or coriander.

**Note** Harissa is a fiery hot North African spice paste made from ground red peppers, chillies, onions and spices. It is available in jars from selected supermarkets and delicatessens.

Serve on a mound of fluffy couscous as a sustaining meal, with extra harissa for added spice if you like.

# Beetroot soufflés with chives

125g/4½oz butter
25g/1oz pecorino cheese, finely grated
70g/2½oz plain flour
450ml/16fl oz milk
salt and white pepper

250g/9oz cooked beetroot, drained
200g/7oz Welsh soft goat's cheese, finely crumbled
4 medium egg yolks
3 tbsp finely snipped fresh chives
6 medium egg whites

**1** Preheat oven to 190C/fan oven 170C/Gas 5. Melt 50g/2oz butter; dice the rest and set aside. Brush 4 individual 350ml/12fl oz soufflé dishes with melted butter and chill for 10 minutes. Brush with butter again and dust with the grated cheese.

**2** Put the diced butter, flour and milk in a pan and whisk on a medium heat until smooth, thickened and bubbling; season very generously (see note). Remove from the heat.

**3** Dice 1 small beetroot and divide between the soufflé dishes, scattering over a quarter of the crumbled goat's cheese.

**4** Put the remaining beetroot in a blender or food processor with the sauce and work to a purée. Add the egg yolks with the remaining goat's cheese and process briefly until just incorporated. Transfer to a bowl and fold in the snipped chives.

**5** Whisk the egg whites in a clean bowl until they form peaks. Fold into the beetroot mixture, a little at a time.

**6** Spoon the mix into the soufflé dishes to within 1cm/½in of the rim. Stand on a baking sheet and cook for 20-30 minutes until risen. Serve immediately.

**Note** It is important to season the soufflé mixture generously as the addition of whisked egg whites will dilute the flavour significantly.

Serve as a sophisticated light lunch, with melba toast and a side salad.

# Baked root layer cake

Illustrated on previous pages

| | |
|---|---|
| 350g/12oz carrots | 2 tbsp lemon juice |
| 350g/12oz parsnip | 85g/3oz butter |
| 350g/12oz celeriac | salt and pepper |
| 2 tbsp clear honey | thyme sprigs, to garnish |

**1** Preheat oven to 200C/fan oven 180C/Gas 6. Peel and coarsely grate the carrots, parsnip and celeriac, using a hand grater or food processor fitted with a coarse grating disc, keeping each vegetable separate. Place in individual bowls.

**2** Warm the honey, lemon juice and butter in a small pan over a low heat until melted. Season with salt and pepper. Pour a third of this mixture over each vegetable and mix well to coat.

**3** Line a shallow 20cm (8in) springform cake tin with non-stick baking parchment. Spoon the carrot into the tin, spread evenly and press down gently. Repeat with the parsnip. Finish with the celeriac, pressing down gently as before.

**4** Cover with buttered foil and bake for 35 minutes, removing the foil for the final 10 minutes to brown the top.

**5** Leave to stand for 10 minutes, then turn out and remove lining paper. Garnish with thyme and serve cut into wedges.

This layered 'cake' of carrot, parsnip and celeriac is perfect with roast meat or game.

# Roasted vegetables with thyme and lemon

**Serves 4–6**

350g/12oz sweet potato, peeled
1 aubergine, trimmed
2 courgettes, cut into chunks
1 red pepper, halved, cored and
  seeded
1 small fennel bulb, halved and
  cored
1 small red onion, cut into wedges
1 tbsp chopped fresh thyme, plus
  3-4 sprigs

4 tbsp olive oil, plus extra for
  drizzling
coarse sea salt and pepper
2 fresh rosemary sprigs
**To finish**
finely grated zest of ½ lemon
2 tbsp chopped fresh flat leaf parsley
25g (1oz) pine nuts, toasted
juice of ½ lemon, or to taste

**1** Preheat oven to 220C/ fan oven 200C/Gas 7. Cut the sweet potato into
4cm/1½in chunks; thickly slice the aubergine and halve each slice; cut the
courgettes into chunks on the diagonal; cut the red pepper into 4cm/1½in
squares; cut the fennel into thin wedges. Put these vegetables into a large bowl
with the onion wedges. Add the olive oil and chopped thyme and toss well.
**2** Transfer the vegetables to a large roasting tin, placing them in a single
layer. Sprinkle with sea salt and pepper, scatter the thyme and rosemary
sprigs on top and drizzle with a little more olive oil.
**3** Roast for about 45 minutes until the vegetables are tender, stirring from
time to time to ensure even browning. Meanwhile, mix together the lemon
zest, parsley and toasted pine nuts.
**4** Transfer the roasted vegetables to a warm serving dish and scatter with
the parsley mixture. Finish with a generous squeeze of lemon juice.

Serve as a light vegetarian main dish or as an
accompaniment to chargrilled meat, such as
lamb chops and steaks.

# Polenta with thyme scented vegetables

1.3 litres/2¼ pints water
salt and pepper
125g/4½oz butter, cut into cubes
375g/12oz quick cook polenta
2 egg yolks, beaten
100g/4oz pecorino or Parmesan
  cheese
8 tbsp extra virgin olive oil
1 onion, finely chopped
4 garlic cloves, crushed

1 red pepper, cored, seeded and
  chopped
4 fresh thyme sprigs
175g/6oz small okra, tips trimmed
250g/9oz patty pans or courgettes,
  halved
2 large tomatoes, skinned and
  chopped
thyme sprigs, to garnish

**1** To make the polenta, bring the water to the boil in a pan. Add salt and half of the butter. Take off the heat and pour in the polenta, whisking constantly. Continue to whisk over a low heat until thick. Off the heat, whisk in the egg yolks and two thirds of the cheese. Tip on to a dampened baking tray and spread to an even thickness, about 1.5cm/⅝in. Leave to cool. Melt remaining butter.

**2** Heat 4 tbsp oil in a large pan and fry the onion and garlic until softened. Add the red pepper and thyme sprigs; cook for 5 minutes. Lift out the vegetables with a slotted spoon.

**3** Heat remaining oil in the pan and stir-fry the okra over a high heat for 2 minutes. Add the patty pans and cook, stirring, for 2 minutes. Add the onion mixture, tomatoes and seasoning. Lower the heat and cook for about 4 minutes; the vegetables should retain a bite.

**4** Preheat oven to 200C/fan oven 180C/Gas 6. Cut the polenta into triangles; arrange overlapping on baking sheets. Brush with melted butter, scatter with remaining cheese and bake for 10-20 minutes until golden. Serve the polenta topped with the vegetables and fresh thyme.

Serve as an accompaniment to grilled meats, or as a vegetarian main course.

# Caramelised new potatoes with orange

Illustrated on previous pages

900g/2lb new potatoes, scrubbed
salt and pepper
2 fresh mint sprigs
50g/2oz butter
2 tbsp fine cut Seville orange
  marmalade
1 tbsp finely chopped fresh mint

**1** Add the potatoes to a large pan of boiling salted water with the mint
sprigs and cook for 7-10 minutes, depending on size, until almost tender.
Drain well; discard the mint.
**2** Melt the butter in a wide based pan, add the potatoes and shake the pan
to coat the potatoes in the butter.
**3** Add the marmalade and heat gently to melt it, turning the potatoes to coat
well. Cook for about 15 minutes, stirring, until golden brown and caramelised.
**4** Toss in the chopped mint and serve.

New potatoes with a sweet hint of marmalade
to partner duck, chicken and pork.

# Indian potato and sweetcorn salad

700g/1lb 9oz potatoes (preferably
   Desiree), peeled and cut into
   2.5cm/1in cubes
2 tbsp vegetable oil
6 spring onions, finely sliced
2 tsp cumin seeds
1 tsp hot paprika

two 340g cans sweetcorn niblets,
   drained
juice of 1 lemon
½ tsp garam masala
3 tbsp chopped fresh coriander
   leaves
salt

**1** Cook the potatoes in lightly salted water until tender. Drain and set aside.
**2** Heat the oil in a large frying pan and stir-fry the onions for 1-2 minutes.
Add the cumin seeds; fry, stirring, for 30 seconds.
**3** Add the paprika, potatoes and sweetcorn. Heat through, then stir in the
lemon juice and garam masala. Take off the heat and gently stir in the
coriander. Season with salt and serve warm, or at room temperature.

Paprika, cumin and lemon juice give this
unusual side salad a piquant flavour.

# Fennel, endive and lime salad

Illustrated on previous pages

2 Florence fennel bulbs (with fronds)
100g/4oz curly endive
**For the dressing**
finely grated rind and juice of
   2 limes
6 tbsp extra virgin olive oil

2 tbsp finely shredded fresh basil
2 tbsp finely diced pitted Greek
   black olives
2 sun-dried tomatoes in oil, drained
   and finely chopped
salt and pepper

**1** Mix the dressing ingredients together in a large bowl and set aside.
**2** Trim the fennel, discarding the stalks but reserving the feathery fronds.
Halve and core the bulbs, then finely slice, using a mandolin or very sharp
knife. Immediately toss the fennel slices in the dressing and leave to
marinate for 15 minutes.
**3** Add the curly endive and reserved fennel fronds to the marinated fennel,
toss gently to mix, then transfer to a clean salad bowl. Serve immediately.

**Note** To prevent discoloration, toss the fennel in the dressing as soon as
it is sliced and don't marinate the salad for longer than stated in the recipe.

Wafer-thin slices of fennel are marinated in a
citrus dressing to soften, then combined with
crisp curly endive for a refreshing side salad.

# Avocado and red chilli salad

**Serves 3-4**
2 large or 3 small ripe avocados
2 bananas
2 tbsp lemon juice
1 tsp very finely chopped red chilli
50g/2oz walnuts, roughly chopped
salt and pepper
1 tbsp finely shredded coriander
    leaves

**1** Peel the avocados and bananas, then cut into bite size pieces, discarding the avocado stone. Place in a bowl.
**2** Immediately toss with the lemon juice, chilli, walnuts, seasoning and coriander. Serve at once, with wholemeal bread.

An unusual medley of flavours makes this a lively, nutritious salad.

# smart
# desserts

# Pecan and maple syrup baklava

**Makes 12-20 squares**
225g/8oz shelled pecan nuts
50g/2oz light muscovado sugar
½ tsp ground mixed spice

400g/14oz packet large filo
  pastry sheets
140g/5oz butter, melted
175g/6oz maple syrup, warmed

**1** Preheat oven to 220C/fan oven 200C/Gas 7. Grease a shallow 28x18cm/ 11x7in baking tin.

**2** Coarsely grind the pecan nuts in a food processor, then transfer to a bowl. Add the sugar and mixed spice and stir to mix.

**3** Unroll the filo pastry and cut in half widthways to make 2 rectangles. Place one half on top of the other and cover with cling film to prevent the filo pastry drying out.

**4** Lay one sheet of filo in the tin, allowing it to extend up the sides. Brush with melted butter. Layer five more pastry sheets on top, brushing each with butter and trimming to fit the tin. Sprinkle with a fifth of the nut mixture.

**5** Repeat this process four more times, to give five layers of nut mixture. Cover with five more sheets of pastry, brushing each with melted butter and trimming the pastry to fit as you go.

**6** Mark the surface of the baklava into 12-20 squares with the tip of a very sharp knife. Bake for 15 minutes, then lower the setting to 180C/fan oven 160C/Gas 4 and bake for a further 10-15 minutes until golden.

**7** On removing the baklava from the oven, spoon the warm maple syrup over the surface. Leave to cool in the tin for about 2 hours. Using a sharp knife, cut into the marked squares to serve.

Crisp, light filo pastry layered with a mildly spiced pecan nut mixture and drizzled with maple syrup.

# Walnut beignet with a coffee cream filling

Illustrated on previous pages

**Serves 6**

**For the walnut paste**
200g/7oz walnut pieces
50g/2oz caster sugar
1 large egg

**For the choux pastry**
65g/2½oz plain flour
50g/2oz unsalted butter
150ml/¼ pint water
2 tbsp caster sugar
2 large eggs, lightly beaten

**For the coffee cream**
1 tbsp espresso coffee powder
25g/1oz light muscovado sugar
75ml/2½fl oz water
300ml/½ pint double cream
2 tbsp Tia Maria (optional)

**To finish**
icing sugar, for dusting

**1** Preheat oven to 220C/fan oven 200C/Gas 7. Grease a 20cm/8in spring-release cake tin. Set aside 50g/2oz walnuts. Whizz remaining nuts in a food processor until finely ground. Add the sugar and egg; blend to a soft paste.

**2** For the choux pastry, sift the flour onto a sheet of greaseproof paper. Heat the butter, water and sugar in a pan until melted, then bring to the boil. Take off the heat, tip in the flour and beat well until the mixture leaves the side of the pan. Cool for 2 minutes.

**3** Beat in the eggs, a little at a time, until smooth and glossy. Spread half the mixture in the prepared tin and dot with the walnut paste. Spread the remaining mixture over the top and scatter with the reserved walnuts, pressing them in gently.

**4** Bake for 20 minutes until well risen, then reduce setting to 190C/fan oven 170C/Gas 5 and bake for a further 10 minutes until crisp and golden.

**5** Meanwhile, for the coffee cream, gently heat the coffee, sugar and water in a small pan for 5 minutes. Strain through a fine sieve into a clean pan. Add the cream and cook for 3 minutes until slightly thickened.

**6** Dust the pastry with icing sugar and serve warm, with the coffee cream.

# Treacle and orange tart

**Serves 8**

**For the filling**

2 small whole oranges

500g/1lb 2oz golden syrup

85g/3oz hazelnuts, finely chopped

85g/3oz white breadcrumbs

2 tbsp lemon juice

2 large eggs, beaten

**For the pastry**

225g/8oz plain flour

140g/5oz unsalted butter, diced

1 egg yolk

1 tbsp caster sugar

2 tbsp cold water

**1** Put the oranges in a small pan, just cover with boiling water and simmer gently for 30 minutes or until the skins are soft. Drain; leave to cool.

**2** To make the pastry, blend the flour and butter in a food processor until the mixture resembles breadcrumbs. Add the egg yolk, sugar and water. Mix briefly to a smooth dough. Wrap and chill for 30 minutes.

**3** Preheat oven to 200C/fan oven 180C/Gas 6. Roll out the pastry on a lightly floured surface and use to line a 25cm/10in loose-bottomed flan tin, 4cm/1½in deep. Line with greaseproof paper and baking beans and bake blind for 15 minutes. Remove paper and beans; bake for a further 5 minutes.

**4** Halve the cooked oranges, discard any pips and blend to a purée. Warm the golden syrup in a pan until slightly thinned. Stir in the nuts, breadcrumbs, orange purée and lemon juice, then the eggs.

**5** Turn into the pastry case and bake for about 30 minutes until the filling is pale golden but not firmly set. Allow to cool slightly before serving.

Puréed oranges give this tempting deep treacle tart a wonderful tangy flavour.

# Coconut and mango meringue pie

Illustrated on previous pages

**Serves 8**

175g/6oz plain flour
85g/3oz unsalted butter
3 large egg yolks
25g/1oz caster sugar

**For the filling and topping**

2 medium, ripe mangoes, peeled

2 tbsp cornflour
150ml/¼ pint orange juice
200g/7oz caster sugar
3 large eggs, separated
85g/3oz creamed coconut,
  finely grated
toasted coconut shavings (optional)

**1** To make the pastry, put the flour and butter in a food processor and process until the mixture resembles fine breadcrumbs. Add the egg yolks and sugar and work briefly to a firm dough. Wrap and chill for 30 minutes.

**2** Preheat oven to 200C/fan oven 180C/Gas 6. Roll out the pastry thinly on a lightly floured surface and use to line a 20cm/8in loose-bottomed flan tin, about 4cm/1½in deep. Bake blind for 20 minutes, then remove paper and beans and bake for a further 5 minutes. Increase setting to 220C/fan oven 200C/Gas 7.

**3** Slice 1 mango, discarding stone; arrange in the pastry case. Purée the flesh from the other mango in a blender until smooth.

**4** In a pan, mix the cornflour with 2 tbsp orange juice to a smooth paste. Add the remaining orange juice, mango purée and 25g/1oz sugar. Bring to the boil, stirring until thickened, then take off the heat and cool slightly. Beat in the egg yolks. Turn the filling into the pastry case.

**5** For the meringue, whisk egg whites in a clean bowl until stiff. Gradually whisk in the remaining sugar, a spoonful at a time, until the meringue is stiff and glossy. Carefully fold in the grated coconut, then spoon over the filling. Bake for 5-10 minutes until the meringue is golden. Cool before serving, topped with coconut shavings if liked.

An exotic version of lemon meringue pie.

# Mocha fudge torte

**Serves 6-8**
140g/5oz plain chocolate, in pieces
85g/3oz butter, cut into cubes
85g/3oz ground almonds
3 medium eggs, separated
85g/3oz caster sugar
1 tbsp coffee powder

**For the syrup**
24 coffee beans
85g/3oz caster sugar
100ml/3½fl oz water
4 tbsp kalhúa or other coffee liqueur

**1** Preheat oven to 180C/fan oven 160C/Gas 4. Line the base of a loose-bottomed 20cm/8in cake tin with greaseproof paper. Melt the chocolate in a heatproof bowl over a pan of simmering water. Add the butter and leave until melted. Remove from the heat and stir in the ground almonds.
**2** Whisk the egg yolks, caster sugar and coffee powder together in a large bowl, using an electric whisk, until thickened. Add the chocolate mixture and fold in.
**3** Whisk the egg whites in a clean bowl until stiff, then gently fold into the mixture. Pour into the prepared cake tin and bake for 30-40 minutes until crusty on top; it should still be slightly soft in the middle. Leave to cool in the tin, then remove.
**4** For the syrup, put the coffee beans, sugar and water in a heavy based pan over a low heat until the sugar is dissolved, then increase the heat and boil for 5 minutes until syrupy. Add the liqueur and pour into a bowl; cool. Cover and chill until required.
**5** Serve the torte, cut into wedges and drizzled with the coffee syrup.

**Note** Make the torte a day ahead for convenince and keep chilled until ready to serve.

An irresistible, gooey dessert enhanced with a rich coffee liqueur syrup – best served with pouring cream.

# Chocolate star anise cake with coffee syrup

**12 slices**
225g/8oz good quality plain
 dark chocolate
115g/4oz unsalted butter
4 large eggs, plus 2 egg yolks
115g/4oz caster sugar
50g/2oz plain flour, sifted

2 tsp ground star anise
50g/2oz fresh white breadcrumbs
**For the syrup**
300ml/½ pint strong black coffee
115g/4oz caster sugar
2 tbsp kahlúa or other coffee liqueur
1 star anise

**1** Preheat oven to 190C/fan oven 170C/Gas 5. Grease and base line a deep
20cm/8in round cake tin. Melt the chocolate and butter together in a bowl
set over a pan of gently simmering water. Let cool slightly.
**2** Put the eggs, egg yolks and sugar in a bowl and whisk until pale and
thickened. Sift the flour and star anise over the mixture. Add breadcrumbs
and melted chocolate, and fold in carefully using a large metal spoon.
**3** Spoon the mixture into the prepared tin and level the surface. Bake for
35 minutes or until a skewer inserted into the centre comes out clean.
**4** Meanwhile, make the syrup. Put the coffee and sugar in a heavy based
pan and heat gently until the sugar is dissolved. Increase heat and boil for
5 minutes until reduced and thickened slightly. Stir in the coffee liqueur
and star anise; keep warm.
**5** Pierce the surface of the cake with a skewer, then drizzle over half of the
coffee syrup. Set aside to cool. Serve cut into wedges, with the remaining
coffee syrup and crème fraîche.

**Variation** Replace star anise with the crushed seeds from 3 cardamom pods.

**Note** Ground star anise is available from selected supermarkets and Asian
food stores. Alternatively, buy whole star anise and grind them yourself,
using a spice grinder or pestle and mortar.

A superb chocolate cake, flavoured with star
anise and soaked in a coffee syrup as it cools.

# Pear, pine nut and lemon strudel

Illustrated on previous pages

**Serves 4**
2 ripe pears
finely grated rind of 1 lemon
2 tbsp lemon juice
50g/2oz unsalted butter
85g/3oz pine nuts

50g/2oz white breadcrumbs
25g/1oz light muscovado sugar
70g/2½oz clear honey, such as
   orange blossom
100g/3½oz filo pastry
icing sugar, for dusting

**1** Preheat oven to 200C/fan oven 180C/Gas 6. Peel, core and thinly slice the pears crossways. Immerse in a bowl of cold water with 1 tbsp of the lemon juice added.

**2** Melt 15g/½oz butter in a frying pan and fry the pine nuts until pale golden. Add the breadcrumbs and fry gently until golden.

**3** Drain the pears, dry on kitchen paper and put in a bowl with the breadcrumb and pine nut mixture, sugar and lemon rind.

**4** Melt another 25g/1oz butter. Keep one sheet of filo pastry for the topping, well wrapped to prevent it drying out. Layer the remaining filo sheets on a clean surface, brushing each with a little melted butter.

**5** Spoon the filling on top to within 2.5cm/1in of the edges. Drizzle with the honey and lemon juice; dot with remaining firm butter. Fold the short ends over the filling, then roll up, starting at a long side. Lift on to a lightly greased baking sheet, join uppermost.

**6** Brush with any remaining melted butter, then crumple the reserved filo sheet around the strudel. Bake for about 25 minutes until golden. Cool slightly, then dust with icing sugar. Serve warm, cut into slices, with Greek yogurt or crème fraîche.

# Upside down cider apple cake

**Serves 8**

2 Granny Smith's apples
25g/1oz unsalted butter
50g/2oz granulated sugar
115g/4oz butter, softened
115g/4oz light muscovado sugar

grated rind of 1 lemon
2 large eggs, beaten
3 tbsp dry cider
175g/6oz self-raising flour
1 tsp ground mixed spice
50g/2oz sultanas

**1** Preheat oven to 180C/fan oven 160C/Gas 4. Grease the side of a deep 20cm/8in round cake tin (not a loose-bottomed one).
**2** Peel, core and thickly slice the apples. Heat the unsalted butter and granulated sugar in a large, heavy based frying pan until the butter is melted and the sugar starts to brown. Add the apple slices and fry for 1-2 minutes each side until golden. Cool slightly.
**3** Cream the softened butter, muscavado sugar and lemon rind together in a bowl until fluffy, then beat in the eggs, cider, flour, and spice until smooth. Fold in the sultanas.
**4** Arrange the apples over the base of the cake tin, adding any pan juices. Spoon the cake mixture on top and spread evenly. Bake for 30-35 minutes until a skewer inserted in the middle comes out clean.
**5** Leave in the tin for 10 minutes, then invert onto a wire rack and leave to cool. Serve warm.

This is excellent served warm as a pudding, with ice cream or cream.

# Saffron rum babas

**Serves 6**

2 tbsp milk

½ tsp saffron strands

225g/8oz plain flour, sifted

pinch of salt

2 tbsp caster sugar

1 tsp fast action dried yeast

2 large eggs, lightly beaten

50g/2oz butter, melted

**For the syrup**

100g/3½oz granulated sugar

6 tbsp rum

1 tsp pomegranate syrup

**To serve**

lightly whipped cream

1 pomegranate, seeds extracted

**1** Grease 6 small timbales or baba tins. Heat the milk with the saffron almost to the boil, then set aside to infuse until tepid.

**2** Mix the flour, salt, sugar and yeast in a bowl. Make a well in the centre and add the milk, eggs and butter. Mix to a soft, sticky dough, then beat thoroughly for 5 minutes.

**3** Spoon into the tins, cover loosely with oiled cling film and leave in a warm place for 1 hour or until the dough is risen almost to the tops of the tins; remove cling film.

**4** Preheat oven to 200C/fan oven 180C/Gas 6. Bake for 15 minutes until risen and golden.

**5** For the syrup, dissolve the sugar in 200ml/7fl oz water in a pan over a low heat, then boil for 3 minutes until syrupy. Cool, then stir in the rum and pomegranate syrup.

**6** Unmould babas, cool slightly, then stand in a shallow dish. Pour on two thirds of the syrup and leave to soak for 30 minutes.

**7** Serve the babas drizzled with syrup and topped with cream and pomegranate seeds.

Divine saffron babas, flavoured with a pomegranate and rum syrup.

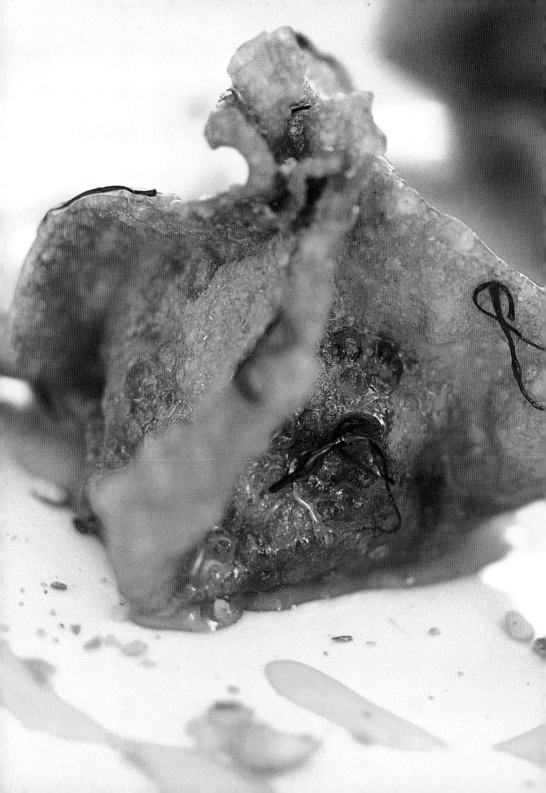

# Date and pistachio wontons

Illustrated on previous pages

large pinch of saffron strands
250g/9oz caster sugar
100ml/3½fl oz water
100g/4oz shelled pistachio nuts

12 medjool dates, stoned and chopped
4 tbsp rosewater essence
12 wonton wrappers
vegetable oil for deep-frying

**1** Put the saffron, sugar and water in a heavy based pan over a low heat to dissolve the sugar. Increase heat and boil for 3 minutes until syrupy.
**2** Put the pistachio nuts in a food processor and process until roughly ground. Remove about one third and reserve for dusting.
**3** Add the dates, 2 tbsp rosewater and 3 tbsp syrup to the processor and work to a paste. Add the remaining rosewater to the syrup.
**4** Put a spoonful of paste in the centre of each wonton wrapper, brush the edges with water and draw up over the filling; press together to seal. Cover with cling film until ready to cook.
**5** Heat the oil in a deep fryer to 170C. Fry the wontons in batches for 30 seconds until golden; drain on kitchen paper. Shortly before serving, reheat the syrup. Bathe the wontons in the hot syrup just before serving.
**6** To serve, put 3 wontons on each plate, drizzle with some of the hot syrup and dust with the reserved crushed pistachios. Serve with crème fraîche.

Fried wontons filled with a scented paste, bathed in a saffron and rosewater syrup, then dusted with crushed pistachios.

# Wild berry roulade

**Serves 6**

**For the sponge**
3 large eggs
85g/3oz caster sugar
70g/2½oz plain flour
15g/½oz cornflour
2 tsp orange flower water

**For the filling**
500g/1lb 2oz mixed soft fruit, such
  as raspberries, sliced strawberries,
  blackberries and redcurrants
3 tbsp pastise, such as Ricard or
  Pernod
1 tbsp clear honey
2 tbsp low fat crème fraîche
2 tbsp yogurt

**1** Preheat oven to 220C/fan oven 200C/Gas 7. Grease and line a 33x23cm/
13x9in Swiss roll tin. Put the fruit in a bowl, add the pastise and honey and
toss gently to mix. Set aside to macerate for about 1 hour.

**2** To make the sponge, whisk the eggs and sugar in a bowl, using an electric
whisk, for about 5 minutes until the mixture is foamy and double in volume.

**3** Sift the flour and cornflour over the mixture, add the orange flower water
and fold in carefully.

**4** Turn the mixture into the prepared tin and spread gently and evenly with
a palette knife. Bake for 8-10 minutes until well risen and just springy to
the touch; do not overcook.

**5** Invert the sponge on to a wire rack, peel off lining paper, then trim the
edges. Lay a clean tea-towel on top and carefully roll up the warm sponge
with the cloth inside; leave to cool.

**6** For the filling, combine the crème fraîche and yogurt in a bowl. Drain
the macerated fruit, reserving the juice, then fold into the yogurt mixture.

**7** Carefully unroll the sponge and remove the tea-towel. Spoon two thirds of
the berry filling evenly over the surface and carefully roll up again. Place
the roulade on a serving dish, with the join underneath. Chill for 1-2 hours
before serving.

**8** Mix the remaining fruit with the reserved juice to make a sauce. Serve the
roulade, cut into slices, with the berry sauce.

A light, airy fatless sponge rolled around
pastise flavoured summer berries.

# Amaretti and apricot tart

Illustrated on previous pages

**Serves 8**
**For the pastry**
175g/6oz plain flour
85g/3oz unsalted butter
3 large egg yolks
50g/2oz caster sugar
**For the filling**
200g/7oz dried apricots, sliced
3 tbsp Grand Marnier or Cointreau
140g/5oz amaretti biscuits, halved
2 large eggs, plus 1 egg yolk

40g/1½oz caster sugar
50g/2oz unsalted butter, melted
300ml/½ pint double cream
300ml/½ pint milk
**For the syrup**
½ tsp saffron strands, soaked in
   1 tbsp boiling water
85g/3oz caster sugar
250ml/9fl oz water
**To finish**
icing sugar, for dusting

**1** To make the pastry, put the flour and butter in a food processor and process until the mixture resembles fine breadcrumbs. Add the egg yolks and sugar and work briefly to a firm dough. Wrap and chill for 30 minutes.
**2** Preheat oven to 200C/fan oven 180C/Gas 6. Roll out the pastry on a floured surface and use to line a 24cm/9½in flan tin, 4cm/1½in deep. Line with greaseproof paper and baking beans and bake blind for 15 minutes. Remove paper and beans; bake for 5 minutes. Reduce to 170C/fan oven 150C/Gas 3.
**3** Soak apricots in liqueur for 15 minutes. Scatter biscuits in the pastry case.
**4** Beat eggs, yolk, sugar and butter together in a bowl. Bring cream and milk to the boil, then whisk into the egg mix. Strain custard into the pastry case, scatter over half of the apricots and bake for 25-30 minutes until set.
**5** For the syrup, dissolve sugar in the water in a pan on a low heat, then boil for 5 minutes until syrupy. Stir in the saffron, remaining apricots and liqueur. Dust the tart with icing sugar and serve with the saffron syrup.

Crushed biscuits and apricots set in a creamy custard within a rich pastry case. A saffron and almond syrup is the perfect complement.

# Plum and almond butter puffs

**Makes 6**

50g/2oz unsalted butter, softened
25g/1oz caster sugar
50g/2oz ground almonds
½ tsp almond extract
340g/12oz ready-made puff pastry

500g/1lb 2oz red plums, halved
  and stoned
beaten egg, to glaze
1 tbsp slivered or flaked almonds
2 tbsp icing sugar

**1** Beat 25g/1oz butter with the sugar, ground almonds and almond extract
to a stiff paste.
**2** Roll out half the pastry on a lightly floured surface and cut out six
10cm/4in rounds; lay on a lightly greased baking sheet. Spread to 1cm/½in
from the edges with the almond paste. Roll out the remaining pastry and cut
out rounds, as above. Position over the filling. With the tip of a sharp knife,
cut a shallow rim, 1cm/½in from the edge of each round. Chill for 30 minutes.
**3** Preheat oven to 210C/fan oven 190C/Gas 7. Cut the plums into thick
wedges and scatter over the pastry rounds, within the cut rim.
**4** Brush the pastry edges with egg, then scatter with the almonds. Bake for
10 minutes until risen and golden. Dot with the remaining butter, dust with
icing sugar and bake for a further 10-12 minutes until deep golden. Serve
with pouring cream.

Ready-made puff pastry rounds sandwiched
with almond paste and baked with a fresh
plum topping for a quick and easy dessert.

# Passion fruit brûlées

4 large egg yolks
¼ tsp vanilla extract
1 tbsp cornflour
2 tbsp caster sugar
284ml carton double cream
2 passion fruit, halved
**For the caramel topping**
8 tbsp caster sugar

**1** Whisk the egg yolks, vanilla extract, cornflour and sugar together
in a bowl until evenly blended.
**2** Heat the cream in a heavy based pan to just below the boil. Pour on
to the egg yolk mixture, whisking all the time. Return to the pan and cook,
whisking constantly, until the custard thickens; do not boil. If the custard
starts to become lumpy, quickly take off the heat and whisk briskly until
smooth, then continue.
**3** Scoop out the seeds and pulp from the passion fruit into a sieve over a
bowl; rub with the back of a spoon to separate the juice from the seeds. Stir
the passion fruit juice into the custard with ½ tsp of the seeds. Pour into
4 small ramekins or other grillproof dishes. Chill for 2-3 hours until set,
or up to 24 hours if preparing ahead.
**4** To make the caramel topping, sprinkle sugar evenly over each custard
and put under a preheated hot grill until the sugar melts and caramelises.
**5** Chill for 2-3 hours until the caramel is set hard before serving.

**Note** If you have a kitchen blow-torch, use this rather than the grill to
caramelise the topping.

Passion fruit adds a refreshing contrast to the
irresistible creaminess of classic crème brûlée.

# Caramelised rice tartlets

Illustrated on previous pages

**Makes 8**
**For the pastry**
225g/8oz plain flour
140g/5oz unsalted butter
4-5 tsp cold water

**For the filling**
40g/1½oz flaked rice
450ml/16fl oz milk
1 vanilla pod
100g/3½oz caster sugar
150ml/¼ pint double cream
2 large eggs, beaten

**1** To make the pastry, blend the flour and butter in a food processor until the mixture resembles fine breadcrumbs. Add the water and process briefly to a firm dough. Chill for 30 minutes.

**2** Preheat oven to 200C/fan oven 180C/Gas 6. Roll out the pastry thinly on a lightly floured surface and use to line eight 9cm/3½in loose-bottomed tartlet tins. Line the pastry cases with greaseproof paper and baking beans and bake blind for 15 minutes. Remove the paper and beans; bake for a further 5 minutes. Reduce oven setting to 180C/fan oven 160C/Gas 4.

**3** Put the rice, milk, vanilla pod and 40g/1½oz sugar in a heavy based pan. Bring to the boil, reduce the heat and simmer gently for about 8 minutes until the rice is tender and the mixture is thickened. Leave to cool slightly. Remove the vanilla pod, then beat in the cream and eggs.

**4** Pour the filling into the tartlet cases and bake for 5-8 minutes until very lightly set. Preheat grill to moderate. Sprinkle the remaining sugar in an even layer over the tartlets and grill for about 4 minutes until lightly caramelised. Serve warm or cold, with sugared raspberries or strawberries.

Tartlet cases with a light, creamy rice filling, baked until softly set, then topped with sugar and caramelised. Best served with berry fruits.

# Meringue roulade with melba fruits

**Serves 8**

**For the meringue**

3 large egg whites

175g/6oz caster sugar

1 tbsp cornflour

2 tsp vanilla extract

1 tsp white wine vinegar

**For the melba filling**

284ml carton double cream

2 tbsp icing sugar, plus extra for
  rolling

2 tbsp peach schnapps or dessert
  wine

1 large peach, peeled, stoned and
  diced

100g/4oz raspberries

**1** Preheat oven to 140C/fan oven 120C/Gas 1. Line a 28x23cm/11x9in Swiss
roll tin with baking parchment.

**2** Whisk the egg whites in a clean bowl until stiff, then gradually whisk
in the sugar, a tablespoonful at a time, until stiff and glossy.

**3** Quickly and carefully fold in the cornflour, vanilla and vinegar. Spoon
into the prepared tin and spread very gently to the edges.

**4** Bake for 35 minutes until set. On removing from the oven, cover the
meringue with a slightly damp tea-towel and leave to cool.

**5** To serve, lightly whip the cream with the sugar and schnapps or wine.
Dust a sheet of non-stick baking parchment with icing sugar. Turn the
meringue onto the paper, then spread with the cream and scatter over the
fruit. Roll up carefully and place on a plate. If preparing ahead, refrigerate
for up to 4 hours until required. Dust with icing sugar to serve.

A luscious mallowy meringue rolled around
a peach and raspberry filling.

# Trio of mango

**Serves 4-6**
300g/10oz caster sugar
juice of 3 lemons
4 large or 6 medium ripe mangoes
300ml/½ pint double cream
425g can lychees in syrup

**1** Put the sugar, lemon juice and 4 tbsp water in a heavy based pan over a low heat until the sugar is dissolved. Increase the heat and boil until syrupy. Allow to cool.

**2** Peel the mangoes, cut the flesh from the stones and put in a blender with the sugar syrup. Whizz to a purée. Transfer 6 tbsp purée to a bowl and reserve for the sauce.

**3** Transfer two thirds of the remaining mango purée to an ice cream maker (if you have one); mix in the double cream and churn according to the manufacturer's instructions. Or pour the purée and cream into a freezerproof container, stir well and freeze for 1½ hours until partially frozen, then turn into a food processor and whizz until smooth. Refreeze, repeat once more, then freeze until required.

**4** For the sorbet, drain lychees over a bowl to catch the syrup. Add the lychees with 150ml/¼ pint of their syrup to the mango purée in the blender and purée. Freeze following instructions for freezing ice cream.

**5** Add the remaining lychee syrup to the mango purée reserved for the sauce. Mix well, cover and chill.

**6** If necessary, soften the ice cream and sorbet in the fridge for 20 minutes before serving. Serve the sorbet in a separate little dish set on a large plate with a scoop of ice cream and a swirl of mango sauce. Scatter with rose petals to decorate, if wished.

This is a perfect finale to a special dinner. Matching fresh rose petals lend a fragrant finishing touch.

# Rosewater pashka

Illustrated on previous pages

**Serves 6**
2 x 250g tubs curd cheese
2 large egg yolks
6 tbsp crème fraîche
2 tsp rosewater essence
50g/2oz butter, softened
50g/2oz caster sugar
85g/3oz chopped mixed candied and
   glacé fruits, such as pineapple,
   cherries and candied citrus peel

25g/1oz raisins
15g/½oz chopped pistachio nuts
**To serve**
few chopped pistachio nuts
orange slices (optional)

**1** Line a 900ml/1½ pint pudding basin with muslin, allowing plenty to
overhang the rim. Tip the curd cheese into a sieve to drain off any whey,
then turn into a bowl. Beat in the egg yolks, crème fraîche and rosewater.
**2** Cream the butter and sugar together in another bowl, then add to the
cheese mixture and beat thoroughly until smooth. Stir in the fruits, raisins
and pistachios.
**3** Spoon the mixture into the lined basin. Cover the surface with the
overhanging muslin, then invert the basin and place muslin side down
on a wire rack over a tray.
**4** Refrigerate overnight, or for up to 3 days if preparing ahead. As the
mixture chills, excess whey drains from the pashka and the texture
becomes firmer.
**5** To serve, remove the pudding basin and muslin. Spoon the pashka on to
serving plates and scatter with pistachios. Serve with orange slices if liked,
and dessert biscuits.

Rosewater adds a floral note to this delectable
Russian dessert.

# Rum punch trifle with exotic fruits

**Serves 6-8**

250g/9oz bought Madeira cake
1 small pineapple, peeled, cored and chopped
1 mango, peeled, stoned and chopped
2 bananas, peeled and thickly sliced
juice and grated rind of 1 lime
juice of 1 orange
3 tbsp icing sugar
90ml/3fl oz dark rum
50g/2oz custard powder
900ml/1½ pints milk
4 tbsp caster sugar
284ml carton double cream, lightly whipped
mint sprigs, to decorate

**1** Slice the Madeira cake and use to cover the base of a large glass serving bowl. Toss the fruits with the lime juice and orange juice, icing sugar and rum, then scatter over the cake.

**2** Blend the custard powder with 4 tbsp milk until smooth. Heat the remaining milk in a heavy based pan until boiling, then whisk into the custard mix. Pour back into the pan, add the sugar and stir over the heat until thickened. Cook, stirring, for 1 minute.

**3** Pour the custard evenly over the fruit and then leave to cool completely. Cover with the whipped cream and chill for 2-3 hours, or up to 2 days if preparing ahead.

**4** Serve topped with the lime rind and mint.

Tropical fruits and plenty of rum give this trifle a Caribbean twist.

# Poached tamarillos with pink panna cotta

Illustrated on previous pages

250g/9oz caster sugar
4 star anise
100ml/3½fl oz grenadine
150ml/¼ pint water
4 tamarillos, stalks intact

450ml/¾ pint double cream
2 tsp vanilla extract
50g/2oz white chocolate
1 tsp powdered gelatine

**1** Put the sugar, star anise, grenadine and water in a heavy based pan over a low heat until the sugar is dissolved. Increase the heat and bring to a simmer.

**2** Cut a cross in the skin at the pointed end of each tamarillo. Add to the sugar syrup, cover and poach gently, turning occasionally, for 10-15 minutes until just soft; test with a skewer. Leave in the syrup for 24 hours.

**3** Meanwhile, make the panna cotta. Slowly heat the cream in a heavy based pan over a very low heat until bubbles start to appear around the edge; this should take 10-15 minutes. Take off the heat and add the vanilla and chocolate, stir until melted.

**4** Measure 150ml/¼ pint of the poaching syrup into a small heatproof dish. Sprinkle over the gelatine, leave to soften for a few minutes, then stand over a pan of simmering water until dissolved. Stir into the cream.

**5** Pour into four 150ml/¼ pint oval darioles or other moulds and chill for 24 hours until set.

**6** To unmould the panna cotta, dip the moulds briefly into hot water, then invert on to plates. Place a tamarillo on each plate and spoon over some of the syrup to serve.

Teamed with panna cotta, tamarillos make a stylish prepare-ahead dessert.

# Sicilian cassata

**Serves 10-12**

350g/12oz bought all-butter
  Madeira cake
150ml/¼ pint cassis or framboise
750g/1lb 10oz ricotta cheese
175g/6oz icing sugar, sifted
150ml/¼ pint whipping cream
250g/9oz ready-to-eat exotic dried
  fruit mix (papaya, pineapple,
  mango and melon), finely diced

100g/4oz glacé cherries, finely diced
100g/4oz dark, bitter chocolate,
  chopped
50g/2oz shelled pistachio nuts,
  chopped
3 tbsp strega liqueur or Marsala
candied or fresh cherries on stalks
  to decorate (optional)

**1** Cut the cake into 1cm/½in thick, long slices and brush one side with cassis. Use to line the side and base of a 23cm/9in spring-release cake tin, placing the brushed sides outwards and trimming to fit the tin as necessary, so there are no gaps. Brush the inside of the case with cassis, then chill.

**2** In a large bowl, whisk the ricotta with the icing sugar together until smooth. Whip the cream in another bowl until it forms soft peaks, then fold into the ricotta mixture.

**3** Fold in the dried fruits, cherries, chocolate and pistachios, then the liqueur. Spoon the mixture into the prepared tin and freeze for at least 10 hours until firm and easy to slice.

**4** Unmould the cassata on to a plate. Cut into wedges and serve each portion topped with a cherry on a stalk if wished.

**Note** If the cassata has been frozen for longer than 10 hours, transfer to the fridge 30 minutes before serving to soften slightly.

An elegant frozen ricotta cake, richly flavoured with exotic dried fruit, cherries, dark chocolate and pistachios.

# Florentine baskets with vanilla ice cream

**Serves 10**

**For the baskets**

50g/2oz unsalted butter

50g/2oz caster sugar

50g/2oz golden syrup

50g/2oz plain flour

25g/1oz mixed crystallised or glacé
   fruit, such as pineapple, ginger,
   cherries and/or angelica

25g/1oz blanched almonds or
   shelled pistachio nuts, chopped

¼ tsp grated lemon rind

140g/5oz plain chocolate, melted

**To serve**

1 litre/1¾ pints good quality vanilla
   ice cream

crystallised violets or ginger,
   to decorate

**1** Preheat oven to 180C/fan oven 160C/Gas 4.

**2** Melt the butter, sugar and golden syrup together in a pan over a low heat. Off the heat, stir in the flour, fruit, nuts and lemon rind; mix well.

**3** Drop 3 or 4 teaspoonfuls of the mixture on to non-stick or greased baking sheets, spacing well apart to allow for spreading. Bake for 10 minutes until golden brown.

**4** Allow the biscuits to cool very slightly until starting to firm up, then quickly lift each one with a palette knife and drape over an upturned dariole mould or small tumbler. Using your fingers, carefully press into a basket shape, fluting the edges.

**5** Repeat with the remaining mixture; leave the baskets until cool and set firm.

**6** Melt the chocolate in a heatproof bowl over a pan of simmering water. Carefully release each basket from its mould, and dip the base into the chocolate to coat. Place the baskets, chocolate side up, on a wire rack and leave until set.

**7** Just before serving, fill the baskets with scoops of ice cream. Top with crystallised violets or ginger to serve.

**Variation** Use good quality white chocolate instead of plain. Dip the rims of the baskets rather than the bases into the melted white chocolate to give an attractive edging.

# Iced pear parfait

**Serves 6**

225g/8oz caster sugar
225ml/8fl oz water
6 ripe flavourful pears, such
   as Comice

4 tbsp poire williams liqueur
300ml/½ pint double cream
1 small egg white

**1** Put the sugar and water in a heavy based pan and dissolve over a low heat, then increase the heat and boil until syrupy.

**2** Using a mandolin or very sharp knife, cut 6-12 very thin slices lengthways from the central part of 2 pears, keeping the peel, core and stalk intact. Lay them in the syrup.

**3** Peel and core the rest of these 2 pears, and the other 4 pears. Roughly chop the flesh and put into a heavy based pan with the poire williams. Cover and cook over a low heat for about 8 minutes until soft, checking to make sure they don't stick. Transfer the pears and liquor to a blender and purée. Turn into a large bowl and cool.

**4** Preheat oven to 110C/fan oven 100C/Gas ¼. Carefully drain the pear slices and lay on a silicone lined baking tray, reserving excess syrup. Put in the oven for 2 hours until crisp, but not coloured. Peel off the paper. Store in an airtight container between sheets of kitchen paper for up to 2 days.

**5** Whip half the cream in a bowl to soft peaks, then fold into the cooled pear purée. In a clean bowl, whisk the egg white until stiff, then add 3 tbsp of the reserved syrup and whisk until glossy. Gently fold into the pear purée.

**6** Spoon the parfait mixture into six 125-150ml/4-5fl oz timbales or dariole moulds, level the tops and freeze for at least 8 hours.

**7** To make the butterscotch sauce, boil the remaining sugar syrup to a golden caramel colour. Take off the heat and then pour in the rest of the cream, taking care as it will splutter; stir well to dissolve the caramel.

**8** To unmould the parfaits, stand moulds in cold water for 30 seconds, invert onto a fish slice and transfer to a tray. Store in freezer until ready to serve.

**9** To serve, warm the butterscotch sauce. Place a parfait on each serving plate and drizzle with butterscotch sauce. Decorate with the pear crisps.

The pear parfaits, wafer-thin pear crisps and butterscotch sauce can all be made in advance.

# Index

## Acknowledgements

The publishers wish to thank the following for the loan of props for photography:
**The Conran Shop**, Michelin House, 81 Fulham Road, London SW3 (0207 589 7401); **Divertimenti**, 139-141 Fulham Road, London SW3 (0207 581 8065); **Divertimenti**, 45-7 Wigmore Street, London W1 (0207 935 0689); **Designers Guild**, 277 Kings Road, London SW3 (0207 351 5775); **Habitat**, 196 Tottenham Court Road, London W1 (0207 631 3880); **Ikea**, Purley Way, Croydon (0208 208 5607); **Inventory**, 26-40 Kensington High Street, London W8 (0207 937 2626); **Jerry's**, 163-7 Fulham Road, London SW3 (0207 581 0909); **LSA International**, The Dolphin Estate, Windmill Road, Sunbury on Thames, Middlesex (01932 789 721); **Muji**, 26 Great Marlborough Street, London W1 (0207 494 1197)

**Food Stylists** Maxine Clark, Joanna Farrow, Marie Ange Lapierre, Louise Pickford, Bridget Sargeson, Linda Tubby
**Photographic Stylists** Kasha Harmer Hirst, Maya Babic
**Contributors** Sara Buenfeld, Maxine Clark, Joanna Farrow, Janet Illsley, Louise Pickford, Bridget Sargeson, Linda Tubby, Sunil Vijayakar